THE
AWAKENING IN
TENNIS

The **BEST MENTAL BOOK**
for **Tennis Players, Athletes,**
Coaches *and* **Parents**

JOSÉ ANTONIO CASARES-FALCONI

BALBOA.
PRESS

A DIVISION OF HAY HOUSE

Balboa Press books may be ordered through booksellers or by contacting:

Balboa Press
A Division of Hay House
1663 Liberty Drive
Bloomington, IN 47403
www.balboapress.com
1 (877) 407-4847

Because of the dynamic nature of the Internet, any web addresses or links contained in this book may have changed since publication and may no longer be valid. The views expressed in this work are solely those of the author and do not necessarily reflect the views of the publisher, and the publisher hereby disclaims any responsibility for them.

The author of this book does not dispense medical advice or prescribe the use of any technique as a form of treatment for physical, emotional, or medical problems without the advice of a physician, either directly or indirectly. The intent of the author is only to offer information of a general nature to help you in your quest for emotional and spiritual well-being. In the event you use any of the information in this book for yourself, which is your constitutional right, the author and the publisher assume no responsibility for your actions.

Any people depicted in stock imagery provided by Getty Images are models, and such images are being used for illustrative purposes only.
Certain stock imagery © Getty Images.

Print information available on the last page.

Scripture quotations marked (NIV) are taken from the Holy Bible, New International Version®, NIV®. Copyright © 1973, 1978, 1984, 2011 by Biblica, Inc.™ Used by permission of Zondervan. All rights reserved worldwide. www.zondervan.com The "NIV" and "New International Version" are trademarks registered in the United States Patent and Trademark Office by Biblica, Inc.™

Scripture quotations marked KJV taken from the King James Version of the Bible.

ISBN: 978-1-9822-3397-6 (sc)
ISBN: 978-1-9822-3396-9 (hc)
ISBN: 978-1-9822-3395-2 (e)

Library of Congress Control Number: 2019913649

Balboa Press rev. date: 09/09/2019

CONTENTS

Acknowledgements vii

Introduction ix

Chapter 1   THE 3 Mental Levels
             (Unconscious & Conscious Players) 1
Chapter 2   THE Present Reality in Tennis.............................23
Chapter 3   How the Brain Works...35
Chapter 4   Successful Minds! 41
Chapter 5   We are Energy. Energy Transforms. Thoughts
             and Words Create. 55
Chapter 6   Mind Over Matter in Tennis 61
Chapter 7   Levels Of Emotions..97
Chapter 8   Training and Competing with Purpose 111
Chapter 9   Your Internal Power (IP)....................................133

Conclusion... 141

ACKNOWLEDGEMENTS

As I start to write this, I ask the Almighty to bless me through the journey of developing this book, and allow me to fulfill my purpose. That my words, concepts, and research from other authors may inspire all readers and help them maximize their potential and build a positive state of mind not only on the tennis court but in their environment and life.

I want to specifically clarify that as I personally see it, all the information presented is a direct expression of True Faith.

> *"He said to them, "Because of your little faith. Amen, I say to you, if you have faith the size of a mustard seed, you will say to this mountain, 'Move from here to there,' and it will move. Nothing will be impossible for you." - **Matthew 17:20 KJV***

Source: **http://www.usccb.org/bible/matthew17:20**

I want to thank my parents, Galo Enrique Casares and Clara Falconi, for guiding me, showing me kindness, teaching me strength with values by the way they have handled themselves in life, and for giving me unconditional love. They taught me the importance of respect, dreaming, and believing in myself and others. I especially thank them for teaching me what faith is and pushing me toward the path that takes me to the light: God. I will never be able to thank you enough! I love you eternally.

I would also like to thank people that I have known and some I don't know who have been molding me and teaching me life lessons through their words, relationships, constructive criticism, advice, books, matches, interactions, videos, conversations, and more.

Thanks to my editors; Donna Mosher and David William Wheeler for giving structure to my manuscript.

Thanks to my sister, Maria Clara, my brother, Galo Adrian, and my two older nephews, JoseMa and Felipe, for giving me life lessons by showing me their fighting spirit every time things got complicated. All of them are warriors and their example has inspired me these last years.

And last but not least, eternal thanks to my wife and best friend, Michelle Moss, for supporting me and pushing me to achieve all my dreams, but most importantly, for showing me the meaning of hard work, true love and faith.

If you like this book; it brings value and has a positive impact on your game, mind and life, please follow the 3x3 rule and recommend this book to three people and ask them to recommend it to three more and so on.

Supporting this mission, will make a change in the tennis industry, other sports and even all teaching industries and Academic Institutions. We will be able to help kids, families, pro-players and teams develop with a better MIND, full of balance and awareness.

INTRODUCTION

When I was very young, I could not comprehend the reason behind a lot of theories, systems, structures and ways of thinking. I could not find a meaning for all the things we did in school. I knew school would give me discipline and structure because I had to wake up early in the morning and do things I didn't like. But I wondered why I had to learn history or mathematics or chemistry, when I thought that information would not help me in my future.

How would I play better during Nationals, or build my own business, by knowing the date when Christopher Columbus discovered the Americas?

Well, now I know it is good to have an education in order to navigate this world and its systems.

But at the time, I asked myself: How can I help my dad improve his architectural business by memorizing the periodic table? How would division or fractions will help me deal with a match point or sell more clothes from my mom's friend? Why do I have to hold the tennis racket a certain way when I'm more comfortable with a different grip that gives me better results? Why should I run towards the ball with short steps when it's not natural and is taking time away from me? How are we so certain about God, His creation, the Big-Bang or Politics when we do not even know how to run a country to properly distribute healthcare, food and shelter for everyone?

At that age, my interests were different from the ones my culture wanted me to focus on.

> "The object of education is not to fill a man's mind with facts, it is to teach him how to use his mind in thinking." – **Henry Ford**

I went to five different private schools, and in all of them I had very good friends. Some of them were disciplined, intelligent and had fantastic grades. Others lacked people skills and common sense, yet still managed to get better grades than most kids.

It was hard for me to understand why my parents had to pay to send me to school when they were able to teach me better lessons for life at home.

As you can tell by now, I've always challenged the "correct" way of doing things.

So now, in tennis, I'm respectfully challenging the system. I wonder why the industry continues to run on a dated program that limits players from reaching their full potential not only technically and physically, but most importantly, MENTALLY.

After graduating college with a major in economics and a minor in business, I worked in corporate America for more than eight years. In that environment, I questioned why I had to do what other people told me when their systems or theories were not efficient.

During my time at a corporation, I learned a lot about business, people, and service, for which I am grateful. However, the best thing I got out of it was the realization that I had to be involved in something I truly love. So I returned to my passion: TENNIS.

For the last 16 years, including the last ten spent coaching tennis, I have studied many successful people and read many books.

Successful people already know much of the information in this book, but it is time for everyone in the tennis industry to have access to it. The information here can be very powerful if you have your mind open. I ask you to please use it for good reasons and with good intentions that will help people and not damage them.

Not only in tennis, but most teaching systems, schools or methodologies do not help people learn how to be aware, to build their dreams, or develop their talents. For that reason, I believe it is my duty to share information that will be able to transform not only tennis, but the way people think and/or teach.

"Small minds discuss people; Average minds discuss events; *Great Minds discuss Ideas.*" – *Eleanor Roosevelt*

1

THE 3 Mental Levels
(Unconscious & Conscious Players)

If you put the teachings of this chapter into practice, not only your game but your life will change forever...

Let's look at three levels of consciousness, or mental levels ranked from low to high:

1. **The Victims:** Excuses & Dark
2. **The Builder:** Actions & Light
3. **The Zone:** Feeling, Flow & Balance -**FFB**

Before we explore how these levels impact your tennis game, let me share with you how a very successful entrepreneur and millionaire, Peter Sage, applies his Four Levels of Awareness to life in general.

I believe these levels are equally applicable to tennis players, coaches, parents, or anyone.

The first level Sage calls "To Me or Victim Mentality." At this, the lowest level, people blame their situations on external factors. "Everything happens TO me." They are victims in all situations. Increasing the level of personal responsibility allows them to move to the second level.

The second level Sage calls "By Me." He says that successful people live in this level because they know that most things, if not all, happen because of their decisions and actions. They have goals and desires, and they persist to achieve them. To move from Level 1 to Level 2, you need to get rid of blame. People at Level 2 take charge of their lives. They know the future happens BY them, not TO them. This level will bring success, but it is exhausting. You are always swimming upstream, when really you want to be in the flow. That means moving to Level 3.

Peter Sage calls the third level "Through Me." In this level, you do not force anything; positive things just happen! Life flows through people in Level 3, and doors open to them naturally.

In order to move from Level 2 to Level 3, you need to get rid of the need for control, allow faith and belief to be part of your life, and trust the bigger picture. You start making magic in your life when you shift from thinking that life happens *to* you to thinking that life happens *for* you.

Source: **https://www.youtube.com/channel/UCCZVmatSqIMTTB8 uExk8xEg**

Sage has a fourth level he calls "As Me." This is when you realize everything is one; everything is connected. Only a few people get to this level. But ideally that's where we all want to be because they key for this level is unconditional Love.

Now I will explain how I have interpreted Sage's Four Levels of Awareness into three levels for the game of tennis.

LEVEL 1
The Victim: Excuses & Darkness

Victims have a habit of blaming people or external factors for their results.

I'm sure you know this level. Maybe you have been a victim as a tennis player. Here are some of the things players at all levels – from the pro level on down – have said about their game.

Do any of these excuses sound familiar? As you read them, consider how shifting this mentality or attitude can change your game – and your life.

- The media and team put too much pressure on me after I won my first Grand Slam, so I can't perform anymore.
- My opponent was too good. She kept hitting winners to the corners and lines so I couldn't play my game.
- My boss stresses me out, and I can't stand him, so I can't get a promotion.
- My opponent was a pusher, and I lose my rhythm with that type of player.
- The line ref was making terrible calls, and I lost concentration.
- It was 5-5 (deuce), and the public kept making noise, so I double faulted and he broke my serve.
- It was too windy, and I couldn't control my shots from one side of the court.
- My toss was not regular, and that affected my serve, so she broke my serve five times.
- My student doesn't listen to me. He is stubborn.
- My child is too shy, and he doesn't have enough fire to compete in high levels.
- My team doesn't offer me what I need because they are not qualified enough for my level.
- My employees are not as passionate as I am, and that's why my business doesn't work properly.
- My coach doesn't tell me what to do when I'm losing during practice!

As you can see, most people involved in tennis (or in life)--coaches, students, players, parents, employees, managers, business owners, etc.--live in the first level of awareness. Therefore, they live in the dark. They can't see reality, they always find something to blame, and they don't take responsibility for their mistakes, actions, or results.

It is important to understand what a Victim gains from being in this state of mind. When a Victim blames someone else for anything that has happened, they are not taking ownership of their actions. When they do this, they want validation from other people. If they get that validation, it will make them feel right. But it gives them absolutely no power in tennis – or life. That is why I call this **a state of darkness.**

When you are in complete darkness, you cannot see. If you can't see, the chances of making good decisions or moving forward decrease dramatically.

Think about a child when he is learning new things. The child is not afraid of making mistakes. When a child is learning to walk, he or she falls hundreds of times. But since their mind is clear and there is no ego or blame, they know they have to keep trying, and sooner or later they will learn to walk. *The miracle of Faith, Believe or Persistence has done the magic.*

Imagine if that baby blamed someone else because he keeps falling down. Do you think the baby will learn to walk? No way!

The child knows UNCONSCIOUSLY that it is up to him to get up and continue his journey and learn… or stay crawling forever. But a child is a child, and the level of consciousness has not been developed that much because of lack of experience. Or maybe his level of consciousness is still pure, therefore, he continues learning without judging anyone or anything, including himself. Or maybe his subconscious is running on autopilot and since he is a sponge, he automatically learns from his mistakes and keeps moving forward. Everything depends how you see things and your perspective.

We will talk about that a lot, about changing the way we see things in later chapters.

However, we adults should be able to stop, think for a second and rationalized before accusing anyone or anything about our actions, results, circumstances and so forth, and make adjustments to keep moving forward.

I'm including below a real-life example that happened to me recently.

ITF International Players:

Two years ago for four weeks, I was at the International Tennis Federation (ITF) Junior Tournaments in Jamaica, Anguilla, the Bahamas, and Panama.

I got to know and talk to three very talented players. They demonstrated nice technique, they were very athletic, big fighters, and they were passionate about the sport. I watched their matches whenever possible.

During the third week, in Nassau, one of them played against seed number one. He lost 6-7/1-6, if I recall correctly. I asked him what happened in the match. He told me he was winning 6-5 (0-30) receiving, but the other kid served a couple of aces, hit some winners, held serve and that was the end. After I heard that I asked him, "What happened in the tie breaker and the second set?" He told me his leg was hurting, and he couldn't play anymore.

I then turned to his friend who was standing next to him, and asked about her match. "What about you?" She said the ref made two bad calls. She was telling the truth because I was watching her match. In her first set, she was 3-3 and with a chance to break the other girl's serve. The referee made a couple of mistakes, and it cost her that game. When I said that I saw the ref's mistakes, she turned to her friend, and said, "You see!"

Her friend said to me, "She is blaming the ref and those two points for the entire match!"

"I agree with you," I said. "She can't blame the entire match on those two situations, but you are doing the same in your match with the aces and your leg. You are doing exactly what she is doing."

They looked at each other, started talking in their own native language which was not English or Spanish so I didn't know what they were saying and they left. I saw them walk away but at the moment I wanted to teach them the 3 levels of mentality because I knew that would help them a lot. Unfortunately, they were not my students, so I decided to respect their coach who is a great, very professional and funny guy from Portugal. I didn't say anything.

If those players learn to abandon the victim mindset, they will be on the right track. Growing and taking ownership of your mistakes is key to keep moving forward.

If you are in the first mental level, it is very hard to find positive results inside or outside the court. **Results do not come from blaming others or external factors. This is a simple but deep concept that everyone knows… but just a few truly understand.**

If external factors are bothering you, you can continue to be bothered or you can make a change in the way you see things or the way you behave. One time I heard somewhere that the best antidote for worry, was action.

The wisdom of Victor Frankl will help you move up to the second mental level:

> "When we are no longer able to change a situation, we are challenged to change ourselves." – **Victor Frankl**

People are not defined by their results; they are defined by their attitude towards what happens to them and how they handle each situation. Remember when Roger Federer lost against Rafael Nadal in the Australian Open and Roger couldn't stop crying?

The memory that stayed with me was not Rafael celebrating his victory but how Rafael reacted towards Roger and gave him a hug when Roger was crying uncontrollably.

The results in that particular final didn't define both players. But the emotions shown, the lesson on how to win, loose and the respect towards each other was fantastic. Both of them were so proper, polite and caring that an instantaneous image has been stamped on our minds forever. No one that witnessed that moment at the stadium or at home watching it on TV, will be able to forget about it. It's almost impossible.

On the other hand, Roger would have never blame some external factor for his lost that day against Rafael. And if he would have blamed something or someone, the respect we have towards Roger would have probably changed a bit.

So now, be honest with yourself--and your players, your kids, and your coach--and decide which path you want to take. The Dark? Or do you want to move up to The Light and start building your results?

The majority of coaches and parents would like players to jump directly from Level 1 to Level 3, which is The Zone; Feeling, Flow & Balance. However, **I believe you must learn Level 2 and become an expert at it**. Then Level 3 will come to you automatically before you even look for it--**as long as you understand life is not about forcing things but it is about accepting things.**

Now, let's talk about Level 2.

> "THE DIFFERENCE BETWEEN A SUCCESSFUL PERSON AND OTHERS IS NOT A LACK OF STRENGTH, NOT A LACK OF KNOWLEDGE, BUT RATHER A LACK OF WILL."
> – Vince Lombardi

LEVEL 2
The Builder: Actions & Light (Results with Discipline & Hard Work)

People in Level 2 have stopped blaming and accusing others for their mistakes, actions, and results. These people are builders, and they know that most results they get are related to the decisions and actions they took and have nothing to do with external factors.

People at this level, take ACTIONS towards their goals. They have the discipline to see themselves and not others when it comes to judging why things are not working.

This type of mentality and way of living allows them to be out of the darkness and have the CLARITY to see reality how it is and this is what I call being in the Light.

Do you think a player in Level 2 will blame the wind, her backhand, his toss, the media, or her coach for her loss?

No way! That player will be conscious that the wind is affecting both players when it blows. She knows she must take correct actions and decide how to use her strokes against the wind better than her opponent to get better results during that match. Adaptation to the circumstances becomes a priority.

The Level 2 player will train hard on his toss, backhand, serve, mental pressure, and so on, until he improves dramatically and knows those are not the factors to blame for his losses.

I can assume most top ten pro players on the tour are at this level. Or at least I hope they are. When they lose matches, I assume again that they analyze themselves and know that they made bad decisions in very important moments, that they didn't handle pressure the best way in certain moments, that they lost focus or just that their opponent played better than they did.

It's simple to see, right? But it's not so simple for the majority of players and human beings to **put into action**.

I believe most players get to this level because of tournament experience or because they have coaches and parents who are already living most of the time in Level 2. Those players know that they can't control the decisions the opponent is taking, but they can control their own decisions.

That is why when TV commentators or coaches say that a player should control the opponent, they are contradicting nature's natural flow.

We can't control external factors, such as the wind, fans, or the opponent and his strategy. Maybe sometimes we can decide to be aggressive, control the point or the center of the court and spaces but that's different than controlling the human being across from us.

Think about nature for a moment. Imagine a big group of wild horses running. There will be some that are running faster because they want to mark their territory and show who the alpha horse is. They will run and compete because it is their nature, but they can't control anything about the horse next to them. They just run as fast as possible to see if they can capture the lead. If they do not win the alpha spot, it does not mean they are not amazing horses. They all are unbelievable, but on that specific day and in that group, one will win.

Similarly, in tennis we can try to control our shots and the ball as much as possible to put the opponent into situations he may not be comfortable with. However, even when players are uncomfortable, they can come up with great shots out of nowhere, so can we really control the opponent?

Not really.

We just have to do our best, like horses do. If you like horses or even if you don't, I truly recommend watching the movie Seabiscuit. It's a story of a pure blood horse that was born and physically didn't met the expectations of the owners. He was not train properly, he had a temper and no one understood the horse. The actual Jockey that was able to ride it and was able to create a connection with Seabiscuit had a background very similar to the horse. His parents send him away during the Great Depression, he was lonely, had a temper, the heart of a champion and fighter and no one understood him but his passion was riding horses. When the jockey met Seabiscuit, they had an instant connection because they were similar and when they started training/riding together no one was able to stop them and they broke so many records even thou in the past no one had faith in them. Watch it. Lots of lessons can be learned from watching that movie.

Going back to tennis, we can only control internal factors, such as our strokes or desire, our decisions. And if we are aware of our decision making, then the chances of getting a better outcome from the match will increase.

At this higher Mental Level, all the previous excuses of a Victim change in the following ways:

From VICTIM to BUILDER
Victim: The media and my team put too much pressure on me after I won my first Grand Slam, so I can't perform anymore.
Builder: The media and my team expect more of me since I won my first Grand Slam. I understand their point of view because I am very talented, I will improve and prove not only to them, but to myself that I can enjoy my first win, and I will give my best moving forward.

Victim: My opponent was too good. She kept hitting winners to the corners and lines so I couldn't play my game.
Builder: My opponent was comfortable hitting in her favorite strike zone. Next time I will use variety, more spin, and depth to prevent the

same situation. I know I can do it, so it's up to me to have a chance to win against her next time.

Victim: My boss stresses me out, and I can't stand him, so I can't get a promotion.
Builder: My boss has no control over my emotions or performance. I'm going to win him over with my dedication and passion for my job until he gives me the chance for a promotion or his boss recognizes all my hard work. If after this, he still doesn't show any changes, I will find a different job within the company and before accepting I will make sure my new manager and I have great professional chemistry.

Victim: My opponent was a pusher, and I lose my rhythm with that type of player.
Builder: I have to remember that the best way to play against a consistent player is to take advantage of short balls and move into the net or bring them to the net. If I just stay back, they will be comfortable. With nice variety, I will have a better chance of winning against that type of player.

Victim: I was playing well, but he started cheating during important points, and I lost my temper.
Builder: Next time I have to remain calm during a ball disagreement. One ball cannot change the entire match, unless I allow it to do so. I will play with less margin of error and will prevent these situations.

Victim: The line referee was making terrible calls, and I lost concentration.
Builder: The line ref is human, and he can make mistakes. It is okay, as long as I stay focused for the next points.

Victim: It was 5-5 (deuce), and the public kept making noise, so I double faulted and he broke my serve.
Builder: When people make noise, I have to remember that the Davis Cup and other sports have crowd noise. Other athletes can concentrate, so I have to learn from them and not allow this to disturb my focus.

Victim: It was too windy, and I couldn't control my shots from one side of the court.

Builder: It was windy, and that affects both players. So, if I use my shots in a smarter way, I have a better chance of winning next time. I will hit faster against the wind and will use more spin when the wind is with me the next time I play in these type of conditions.

Victim: My kids do not listen to me, and their grades in school are terrible.

Builder: I will show more patience while helping my kids with their homework. I will give them compliments about their talents, and with this behavior I'm positive they will start listening to me and improve their grades.

Victim: My backhand stinks, so I couldn't win today.

Builder: I noticed my backhand is not at the same level as my forehand. I will work very hard to improve it, because I want it to become a solid weapon. This also reminds me I have to improve my footwork so I can develop a very powerful inside out forehand.

Victim: My player chokes every time he faces a pressure moment in the match.

Builder: I'm going to make my player train in pressure situations on a daily basis so she gets used to them. This will allow her to manage stress during matches much better. I trust her confidence level will keep improving day by day.

Victim: My restaurant is not successful because the chef doesn't cook my menu correctly.

Builder: I'm going to trust my chef and allow him to develop the restaurant's menu, because that is why I hired him. My job is to supervise him, not to tell him what to cook or how. If this doesn't work, I will find a better chef or get a successful restaurant owner to be my mentor, so I can succeed.

Victim: My student doesn't listen to me. He is stubborn.

Builder: I'm going to try a different approach with my student, because I know he is talented. I will find a way to motivate him, and this will help us work as a team and solid unit.

Victim: My child is too shy, and he doesn't have enough fire to compete in high levels.

Builder: I have to understand that every child is different and there are explosive, loud, quiet, and peaceful warriors. I will help my child to maximize his skills without trying to change his personality, which is a natural gift. Patience is a gift.

Victim: My weight is not ideal, but on every corner, I see junk food. It is tempting, and I end up eating it.

Builder: Since I want to be in better shape, I will buy organic and natural fruit to prepare to take with me. If I get hungry, I can eat it instead of making a bad choice with fast food and this will also bring me a healthy and long life.

Victim: My student is afraid of losing, and also of winning, sometimes.

Builder: I have to remember that when I was younger, I got very nervous in those situations. I will make sure to communicate to my student that winning is part of the game, but it is most important to learn from every match.

Victim: My team doesn't offer me what I need because they are not qualified enough for my level.

Builder: My team has taught me so much. I will communicate with them and let them know what I think I need to improve so we can come up with a new plan for this coming months.

I'm pretty sure you understand my point of view by now.

Below I have a quick exercise in order to see if you fully understand the concept.

Read the five "Victim" comments below. Complete them by adding the "Builder" version.

- My doubles partner stinks. He doesn't have a solid serve or volleys, so we can't compete aggressively.
- My backhand slice is not good enough for high performance levels, and I can't hit drop-shots.

- My employees are not as passionate as I am, and that's why my business doesn't work properly.
- I'm too slow and not athletic enough to play college tennis.
- I hate my job even though I have a great salary and great health benefits.

> "TO EVERY ACTION THERE IS AN EQUAL AND OPPOSITE REACTION." – Isaac Newton

In the second mental level, people will find ways to get results by working harder than the average human being. People at this level start believing that every positive action has a positive reaction and they start building their future by using the present correctly.

This level will bring results, but it could be stressful, physically and emotionally draining due to all the extra hard work you have to put in on the court and off it.

Before I end this level, I will share a real life story that will clarify even more what I'm trying to communicate.

CALL CENTER

My first job out of college was in a computer sales call center. After I was trained and after some rookie mistakes, I understood how the system worked and clear about how I was going to handle the opportunity. I remember thinking that if someone was calling, it was because they WANTED to buy a computer.

It was my job to help them buy it during their first call. My thought process was: *"If I didn't close the sale during the call, I was sure I made a mistake"*. I was convinced that if they were calling is because they needed a computer. It was very simple.

I remember other sales representatives blaming the quality of the calls, saying that customers were calling just to ask questions and that they didn't have money to buy. Those were their excuses why they didn't hit their monthly quota. Some of them told me I was lucky to receive all these calls from customers that wanted to buy. It wasn't luck. It was my way of seeing things that gave me "quality calls" that brought positive results. I was selling more computers with higher margins and upgrades than most of my co-workers and hitting and exceeding my sales quota consistently. But that's not it.

The most important lesson is that my mentality not only allowed me to sell more but allowed me to get promoted to Marketing and later on to other positions and have a very successful career in that company for the time I spent there.

ONE good decision or a POSITIVE mentality changed SEVERAL situations that showed up in my future.

As a quick summary, if you understand Level 2, you will automatically realize that any individual can't control the calls he receives. However, he can control his attitude or mentality towards the calls he receives, and this will bring positive results.

LEVEL 3
The Zone: Feeling, Flow & Balance (FFB)

> "Trust your instincts. Intuition doesn't lie." – **Oprah Winfrey**

People at this level are **the exception**. Most of them run on a high consciousness level and *understand that life happens FOR them and not to them.*

They accept what it is. Believers would say they accept the will of God. These people are not obsessed about achieving tangible results, but intangible results. They focus on their passion and personal growth. They want to contribute to others and make an impact in this world without forcing things.

> "The glory is being happy. The glory is not winning here or winning there. The glory is enjoying practicing, enjoy every day, enjoying to work hard, trying to be a better player than before." – **Rafael Nadal**

Even though their main focus is NOT tangible results, they actually get what they want because they act based on instinct and follow their natural talents without forcing things. When all these concepts are clear in your head and you live ruled by this mentality, being in The Zone is not only a tennis expression. It applies to your life.

We can see in the quote above how clear this concept is inside Rafael's head and based on his behavior at all times, you know for a fact this is the way he lives. It's a life style. Is not luck that he has been able to reach hundreds of millions of fans with his passion, style, respect, fighting spirit and we can name a long list of qualities he has.

You could never imagine a Rafael in the 1st Mental Level, as a victim. It's just not him. He knows it is not about excuses or winning. It's about intangible things. Joy, Personal Growth, Improvement.

I have never seen Rafael throw the racket or say a bad word towards anyone. That's who he is. A noble, big heart warrior that loves what he does and respects other and himself.

However, I doubt Rafael knew how to play like he plays now. I can imagine he had to move from the dark to the light, become a builder when he was a teenager and now moves from level 2 to level 3 and vice versa.

Most people at this third level, without consciously trying, have been able to change the world. Others have had the goal of changing and helping the world since an early age.

These human beings follow their passion and are obsessed about **improving themselves** and their environment. Since they are so dedicated to their passion, they have a huge impact on average people. People follow their example and respect them immensely. All of them know they have a specific purpose and their mission is to inspire or contribute.

> "I think in life you should work on yourself until the day you die."
> – Serena Williams

Most of these people contribute to humanity with their inventions, art, science, creativity, architecture, business, acting, performances, behavior, speaking, and so on.

They all understand that here on earth, we have "natural laws" that should be followed, whether they are physical, emotional, biological, spiritual, or even structural laws. They show extraordinary respect toward everything. Some of these people are great visionaries: their minds are able to create new concepts, and usually they go against the rules previously established by their culture.

> **"THE MEANING OF LIFE IS TO FIND YOUR GIFT. THE PURPOSE OF LIFE IS TO GIVE IT AWAY." - *Pablo Picasso***

Some recreational or junior players have never experienced The Zone. Sometimes the Zone lasts for a few games and then it goes away. When you are in the zone, you are allowing your true self to play. There is no noise in your head, you already have learned to think and you are such a good builder than you have created a habit to adapt and build anytime you need to.

It is like learning a new language. You practice and practice so much, then all of the sudden, you realize you are not thinking while talking in the new language. The words just come out. The new language is part of you.

Or when you are learning Algebra or Calculus. At the beginning you have to focus so much not to make a mistake. You practice and do so many exercises that you get used to it and all of the sudden you do it on autopilot. It simple to see this.

In tennis we can see that building phase when a kid is learning a technical motion. The coach repeats to the player so many times how to prepare, impact the ball or how to finish the stroke that the player has no option than to repeat the same inside his head and execute what has been ask over and over again until one day all of the sudden, the nice follow through appears out of nowhere and the player doesn't have to remind himself to do it anymore. The follow through becomes part of him, part of his game, part of his essence.

That is a technical situation, however when technical bases are solid and if we talk about concentration, decision making, being in the zone and the good stuff that players need in the moment of truth, how in the world a junior player will be able to get in the zone if he or she never trains in an environment that allows them to get in the zone?

Even when players have solid technical foundations, there are always corrections coming from all angles. Move faster, prepare on time, spin more, don't rush, etc.

The player is always <u>focused on what he is doing wrong</u> rather than what he should, **the ball AND where to hit the ball**. This is essential during the execution of a tennis shot.

The main Purpose. Finding the Ball, connecting with it, deciding what to do with it. Aiming. Just like a sniper or a CEO, **the focus should be on the target**. That's it.

Once players have solid basics they need to train over and over again in order to have the chance to get inside the zone during training. When competition comes and they are not used to silence and the conditions a tournament bring, how will they perform?

They are used to inner-noise. Criticism, corrections, change of thoughts. **There is no clear PURPOSE**.

It's like going to a calculus exam without doing any exercises to practice the days or months before. If you are not pretty much a genius or someone that mathematics comes very easy to, then probably you will fail.

This is what happens generally speaking. The players that have that extra natural gear and are able to focus during competition and it's easy for them to execute a basic strategy, those are the ones that win.

Those are the players that are consistent even if they face someone better than them. Even if the opponent's parents, coach or the public are making noise.

Those are the players that are considered champions. But what about all the rest? Should we give up on them?

I heard on TV from Sloan Stephens when she won the US Open that when she was about 11 years old, her mom and Sloan went to a tennis academy and the head coach said that Sloan will play Division II College if she was lucky.

Can you imagine if Sloan and her mom would have believe what they heard? I'm sure Sloan's mom was a builder at the time or maybe she was already in the 3rd mental level and that's why they continue to follow their dream and purpose.

Most people know by now that hard work wins against talent. But in the sport of tennis I'm not sure if the hard work that most players go through is quality work. Especially in terms of training the mind and allowing the player to be in the zone and reach that feeling on a daily basis.

Even during the first days or months of a beginner player not older than 8, when you are teaching technique, you can automatically train their mind and force them to get in the zone by doing specific drills that accomplish that.

For example, before starting the Drill, I give them **patterns described below** to memorize.

If I say 1 they say 3 and vice versa
If I say 2 they say 4 and vice versa
If I say 5 they say 7 and vice versa
If I say 6 they say Kuack-Kuack and vice versa
If I say 8 they say 10 and vice versa
If I say 11 they say dot.com and vice versa

Once they memorized them, I start the drill and while I hand-feed the ball I choose a number or word and they not only have to respond to the number or word that corresponds to the pattern I chose but they also have to turn/prepare correctly before they hit, then they need to put the ball inside the gigantic square (the court), they have to follow through, freeze the racket at their follow through and shuffle three times before dropping the racket and going back to the line.

If you have never seen this, you would hesitate the little 7 year old kids can do all this at the same time, but they do it and the do it amazingly. Better than any adult could, because they do not have egos or mental obstacles.

Obviously not all follow instructions and do it perfectly the first times but after a couple of reminders they do entire baskets without making any mistakes at all.

If you have read the entire first chapter, **welcome to the Awakening....** probably now is a good time to read and analyze how most people see the sport of tennis at the present moment.

> "If you want to find the secrets of the universe, think in terms of energy, frequency and vibration." – **Nikola Tesla**

2

THE Present Reality in Tennis

Technique, Fitness, Tactics, and Mind

> "It is not the actions and behavior of the good man that should be matched but his point of view. Outer reforms are useless if the inner state is not changed. Success is gained not by imitating the outer actions of the successful but by right inner actions and inner talking."
> — **Neville Goddard**

One of the purpose of this book is to help people see tennis, other sports, and especially life; a bit differently than what they are used to. The world keeps evolving and it is imperative we continue to evolve with it and adapt accordingly.

Is there a magic technical, physical or tactical trick to become a champion? Sadly, we all know there are no magic tricks that will make players into champions.

TECHNIQUE

You may think the term *technique* in the tennis world refers to how players move the racket before, during, and after contact with the ball. I would like to refine the term into one that will be useful for tennis players.

"Technique" means how you use physical body movements to execute your game skillfully and to hit the ball efficiently, with control and power.

Specific technical changes can help you improve and maximize your strokes.

Some professional coaches work with both amateur and professional players on small, technical changes that may increase the RPMs on first serves, reduce the margin of error on groundstrokes, increase the percentage of second serves, and so on.

Tennis is a very technical sport, but it is not as complicated as some. Tennis is more forgiving than many other competitive sports.

Consider figure skating, diving, gymnastics, or swimming. In these sports, if you make a technical mistake, it can mean not advancing to the next round or qualifying for the Olympics.

If your technique is off in swimming, you can lose a quarter of a second, and the race. In diving or figure skating if you make a technical mistake, you can sprain your ankle or even break your back. A technical mistake in these sports, even one as simple as the alignment of your hips and arms, can cost you a gold medal.

Don't get me wrong. I am not saying that in tennis you do not need good technical fundamentals to make it to the highest levels. However, too many coaches and experts only talk about foot work, coordination, body and racket position during point of contact, late preparations, incorrect grips, too much spin or too flat, bad tosses, and so on.

"You are hitting late. Your point of contact is 3 degrees off. You need more rotation or elastic energy. Step into the ball. Watch the ball. Spin it more. Your point of contact is wrong. Move your feet. Stay close to the line. Transfer your weight. Keep the forward momentum. Your timing and feeling is off. Prepare the racket on time. Hit through the ball more. Hit the ball when it is coming up. You should have hit the approach down the line. You should have finished the point."

Most tennis coaches make a living correcting these technical mistakes. I have seen coaches walking behind their professional players telling them what they did wrong and how they can improve technically, physically, or tactically.

During the US Open in 2016, a coach kept telling the player how to toss the ball. This player was ranked in the top 10 in the world. Do you think that player didn't know how to toss the ball?

Do not get me wrong. Technique is important. But what sets apart a Roger Federer, a Rafael Nadal, a Serena Williams, a Novak Djokovic, a Juan Martin Del Potro, a Simona Halep, or an Alexander Zverev?

It is not technique. There is another secret to success, and it is not in the technique.

It is how a player thinks.

Technique plays a huge role in tennis, especially during the initial phases of the learning process. However, have you ever seen two professional or even amateur players with the same technique?

It is impossible, because we all are different. We see similar styles, but that's about it. No players in the world play exactly the same. Good players come from different schools and different teaching methodologies. Every player is different.

FITNESS

Have you ever seen two professional players with the same body? They may share a similar body type and frame, but they are not exactly the same.

There are three different body types: ectomorph, endomorph, and mesomorph. Isner and Del Potro are long and lean ectomorphs. Verdasco and Rafa are muscular and well-built mesomorphs.

Among women, it is more common to see all three types. You will find all in players at the highest levels. Compare Kerber, Serena, Henin, Venus, Sharapova, Navratilova, Chris Evert, Bouchard, etc. They all are built differently. Some of them may even have a mixture of the three body types.

Have you compared the strokes, technically and physically, of players like Goffin or Ferrer against a player ranked 150the in the world? Sometimes low-ranked players have better technical strokes. Some of them are stronger or taller than Ferrer, Goffin, and other top performers. David Goffin is 5'11," 152 pounds. He made the Nitto ATP Finals in November 2017 and is ranked 7th in the world.

Most coaches would say it is now impossible for a male to make it to the top 10 unless he is at least 6'2" and 175 pounds.
But guess what?

The mind makes the difference and everyone knows it but no one wants to talk about it deeply.

Fitness is critical to success in tennis, of course. Improved fitness allows you to get to balls better, use your body mass more, endure longer when matches last for 2, 3 or 4 hours and overall maximize your game.

Experts also explain how if you get physically strong, then you automatically become mentally strong. But some top 200 players are very physically strong and they struggle to get into the top 100 or top 50…Why?

Also, if we think scientifically, we could say that the following formula means a lot:

Force = mass x acceleration ($F = m \times a$)

Diet also gives the body an edge. The human body is a perfect machine and the better and more natural fuel we put in it, the better it will perform. Some triathletes and Ironman competitors have become vegans. They claim they can harness peak performance for more than seven hours of pushing their bodies to the limit. This is a very important topic that has to be studied and become part of the new Tennis Era also.

For example the myth of consuming Carbohydrates before competition **should be debunked** by now after we know so much about food and its benefits or potential risks. Carbohydrates become glucose which pretty much is sugar and the excess consumption can create inflammation everywhere in the body.

Also mixing carbohydrates with Proteins is not ideal for digestion and the Enzymes can't work on what they are supposed to be working which is keeping us healthy and healing things. They have to spend all their energy in digesting. I recommend reading a bit about Keto Reset Diet and one of the pioneers on this topic and way of eating and living, (Mark Sisson) who was a high performance runner but injuries, diabetes and irritable Bowel Syndrome forced him to stop competing. Based on his frustration he started researching and found a way to eat better and heal his body by stopping all the consumption of grains, carbohydrates and sugars. It's amazing and you will learn a lot just from the video below:

Source: https://www.youtube.com/watch?v=k1jXS6Ue3GM

This is a topic I will not develop in this book. Maybe in a different book but its imperative Tennis Players learn how to eat properly and they become students of their bodies. If you do some research you will find what is best for you.

If you study how the body works, you will learn that the cleaner you eat--meaning natural and not processed foods--the clearer the mind will work. Your thought processes and decision-making will improve as well.

A clear example is when Djokovic eliminated gluten from his diet, his performance improved dramatically.

I believe he is more balanced now, but I think the real reason he made changes is that he is focusing on personal growth, which is key for improvement and success.

Then there is Martin Del Potro, who I assume probably enjoys meat and chorizo-sausage like many Argentineans, and he can defeat Djokovic and Rafa at the Olympics in Rio. Funny, eh?

Maybe that specific day in Rio, DelPo used his head and heart a bit more than Nole and Rafa. Maybe Delpo believed more strongly that he could win. Maybe Delpo was strong enough to push away negative thoughts, believing he had nothing to lose after four surgeries? Who knows?

What about Delpo playing against Cilic in the Davis Cup, and coming back from 0-2 sets and playing the fifth set with a broken finger? It's unbelievable what the right state of mind can accomplish.

We would have to get inside their heads to know exactly what they were thinking and feeling at those moments in Rio or Croatia, but we all know that food was not the only factor.

The most important part of fitness is that when a player is fit it has a direct impact on their mental game because it brings confidence.

TACTICS

Some well-known coaches say that tactics create a gigantic difference between average players and high performance players.

In Spain, for example, most coaches tell students to hit their approaches down the line. That makes a lot of sense from the tactical standpoint because you can increase the chances of your opponent hitting crosscourt, therefore you can anticipate to the ball during the first volley.

Some players have patterns of hitting cross court if they are being consistent, and down the line when they want to take control of the point.

Experienced players know these patterns. For example, if you are serving from the even side of the court (15/15) to the forehand of a right-handed player, the chances of them hitting to your backhand are greater. If they hit to the forehand, you can more easily control the point with your stronger shot, and hit down the line or behind a fast player who is trying to return to the center of the court.

Other coaches teach the opposite. They say that if you return to the forehand, the ball travels more distance; so you will have more time to recover. If you hit down the line, you are risking more because the ball will have to travel over the highest part of the net. For that reason, many players now return the serve right to the middle of the court, and deep toward the server's feet, to push the server back and have a chance to start the point without giving too many options to the server.

Coaches see and teach tactical concepts differently. I wonder, who is right? I'm not going to write about all patterns and ways of playing. When it comes to tactics, there are different theories, schools, and points of view.

The real questions are:

When do you apply them? How do you apply them? Do you have the discipline to apply them on every single shot and point? Does tennis allow you to execute them all the time?

In other words, what makes the difference is not necessarily a particular tactic. It is being focus on a purpose and decision making.

The great coach, Paul Annacone, commented on a physically strong young man playing in the Australian Open 2017: "He has to continue to work on his patience, shot selection, power, and knowing when to pull the trigger."

Roger Federer said that if he could change one thing about his game in his early years, he would have liked to have been more consistent.

Rafael Nadal has said that tennis is a sport of mistakes and not of winners.

Sure, we could agree that patience, control, shot selection, and decision making should be priorities.

But when you think a little bit you can ask yourself...Where do decisions, control, patience, and shot selection come from?
Yes! They come from the MIND.

THE MIND

The mind is the key to success in not only tennis, but in every sport--and in life in general.

So, why are players not coached on a daily basis about their mind, their thoughts, and how to get better?

Because most people have no idea how to do it. Also, it is easier to blame footwork, point of contact, shoulder rotation, toss, and so on because the majority of people live in Level 1 (Victims)

Some players and coaches find that professional sports psychologists can help them improve their mental game. I believe that helps, but are players training the mind every day?

Players also look for shortcuts in routines, such as fixing their hair or hat, and moving the bottles and towels in a specific way to "stay in the present." This is an attempt to cheat negative feelings about missing or being nervous, or to cover up any fear about a double fault or missing a shot on a big point.

But such shortcuts to mental success are never consistent, and they do not bring balance and joy to players in the moment of truth or pressure. If you do not face your fears and emotions and you cover them up with routines, the negative emotions stay inside. They could hurt you not only emotionally, but physically.

Injuries in tennis are common, but why? Most people would blame the injuries on overuse or muscle imbalances, but how come some players don't injured as much as others and they play the same, more or very similar amount of hours?

These athletes are built strongly, have good quality training, and can recover quickly. It makes no sense that top players injure themselves so often.

When I was younger and played tennis, you almost didn't see anyone injured. We had different diets, we also didn't even know the word stress existed.

Nowadays, you see junior players younger than 13 and they are already being treated for injuries. It's something to start thinking about and make changes. They level of stress or pressure most players are feeling is causing all these injuries and the pressure affects their mind, emotions and the physical injury is the result of all of this.

Consider this: When you use routines to "stay in the present," it is like asking a cigarette smoker to chew nicotine gum every time he is tempted to smoke, or expecting someone with high levels of cholesterol to take pills instead of improving his diet and giving up fried, fatty foods.

It's madness!
Why, you ask? Many people rely on medication to correct health issues. Yes, and I am suggesting there is a better way. Bear with me, because this may challenge your assumptions. And that is exactly why you are reading this book, right?

To have your assumptions challenged and to learn new ways to improve your game and that's why it is called THE AWAKENING.

For the smoker to stop smoking successfully or the fried food eater to switch to natural, clean food, they have to be aware of their reality, thoughts, tendencies, and addictions. When they consume nicotine and fried food, they are covering up hidden feelings or emotions that have to surface for attention. They must make a *conscious change*. They have to accept that they have developed a bad habit and they need to address the emotions that they are trying to avoid with the habit. When they are aware of the underlying cause that contributes to the hidden feeling, they have a better chance of making changes to progress and become healthy.

It's the same for tennis players. When they are nervous, they have to accept that they are feeling that particular emotion, accept it, and be aware of it – not bury it. For example, if a player can develop the maturity to accept and understand that the outcome of the match does not have anything to do with who they are as a person, then those negative emotions will vanish slowly, but surely.

It is important to understand that not dealing with negative emotions can even bring physical unbalance and lead to physical injuries. Some experts claim that negative emotions can even lead to disease.

Sources: Book called "Healing Back Pain" – Dr. John E Sarno and **https://www.psychologytoday.com/blog/the-athletes-way/201405/negative-emotions-can-increase-the-risk-heart-disease**

"Your Health is your Wealth" – Dr. Robert Sones

In another chapter, I will expand on the power of the mind to influence pain, injuries, strength, and harmony, including the theories developed by Peter Egoscue, an anatomical physiologist. I will also discuss the work of Dr. John Sarno, who wrote about the psychological origins of chronic pain and maintained that most non-traumatic instances of chronic pain — including back pain and headaches— may be traced to deep-seated psychological anxieties. Actually Dr. Sarno's book, HEALING BACK PAIN: THE MIND-BODY CONNECTION, set me on the path to healing my own chronic back pain.

Robert Sones, D.C., supported the theories I learned in Sarno's book. He helped me discover some emotions that were blocking the flow of energy in my body. After only seven sessions, I am now pain-free.

"Whether you are suffering from an acute pain, a chronic illness, a common backache, or just don't feel as good as you would like, you can return to wellness," says Dr. Sones, a pioneer in this work.

He also says the power of the mind to influence the body goes beyond pain. It influences your peak performance, especially in sports.

"The body has an innate inner wisdom," says Dr. Sones. "But the mind can create barriers to top performance. The memory of a past negative experience reduces belief because your body, at the cell level, is running on 'history' instead of the present moment. The undesirable 'historical' event in memory may have occurred yesterday or twenty years ago. The stress hormones associated with that experience are also stored in your sub-conscious memory, ready to re-surface when you least expect it. Not only do you lose focus, you become physically weaker. So you choke. You miss the putt. You fumble the ball. You break your form. History repeats itself because the mind and body are running on a memory. Expressing maximum potential with confidence and focus requires total integration and synchronization at three levels of being: physical, mental, and emotional."

Source: **http://www.drsones.com**

Before I learned the power of the mind to influence performance and health, I spent a lot of money on physical therapy, chiropractic treatments, cortisone shots, acupuncture, and more. I found the best therapy and remedy was getting to know my emotions, how I was feeling, and what I was thinking about certain situations, other people, and myself.

If you think this is crazy, I invite you to research mind-body medicine and psychoneuroimmunology to learn how energy, feelings, and the subconscious mind are connected and how they can impact your health and performance.

I've been preaching to my students for years now that your thoughts and words create your reality. That's not something I invented.

Successful people have demonstrated this through the ages.

*"Take charge of your thoughts, you can do what you will with them." – **Plato***

3

How the Brain Works

There is plenty of information available about how the brain works, its parts, functions and so on. Moreover, neuroscience is discovering new aspects of brain function all the time.

Understanding how the brain works can benefit you in just about any undertaking. When I read a business book[1] by Oren Klaff, an investment banker, I realized his concepts about how the brain works in business could also apply to tennis.

The brain developed in three stages: the "crocodile" or "reptilian" brain; the midbrain, and finally, the neocortex.

Klaff writes that the crocodile brain focuses on survival: filtering incoming messages, generating fight-or-flight responses, and producing basic emotions. The crocodile brain is dedicated to keeping the body alive and has only primitive reasoning power.

The midbrain applies meaning to events and social situations.

The outer part of the brain is the neocortex. It considers complex issues, solves problems, and uses reason to produce answers.

---

[1] Klaff, Oren; Pitch Anything: An Innovative Method for Presenting, Persuading, and Winning the Deal, McGraw-Hill, 2012

Let's look at each of these parts in more detail.

CROCODILE BRAIN

The crocodile brain thinks very simply. It is the first part of the brain to process information coming from another person. It wants to receive information fast, summarized, high contrast, etc. When it receives information, it asks:

- Is this person/thing confronting me?
- Should I run from it?
- Should I kill & eat it?
- Should I mate with it?

MIDBRAIN

The midbrain processes social situations. It is the portion of the central nervous system associated with vision, hearing, motor control, sleep/wake cycles, and temperature regulation.

NEOCORTEX

The neocortex, in the front part of the brain, is in charge of mathematics, linguistics, problem-solving, and so on. It only wants information from the crocodile brain that is new or dangerous. It does not want a problem it has resolved before. This is also the part of the brain that needs more energy to function.

In general, this is the part of the brain that asks:

- Should I talk?
- Should I sleep?
- Should I work?
- Should I attack or defend?
- Should I slice it, or should I hit a drop shot?
- Should I go to the net or stay?

- Should I slow down and hit my first serve in?
- When I play a pusher, do I attack or do I stay consistent?

Players making decisions on the court demand much of the neocortex. At the end of a match, they will not only be physically drained but mentally exhausted as well.

The interaction of the crocodile brain with the neocortex requires repetition of instruction and practice of the technique before a player will remember how to perform it. It is exhausting. A player will drain themselves just thinking, WHAT SHOULD I DO? Once the brain remembers the "correct" answers to the question "What should I do" repeatedly, then the answers or actions become habit and a part of mind-memory or muscle-memory.

This is very important to understand, especially if you are a tennis coach and have high expectations for your students.

It also is one of the reasons some coaches want the players NOT to think and just play on autopilot. However, in tennis (and in life) it's not that simple to be on autopilot when another person is "controlling" the situation.

For example, let's say Player X is 12 years old, and he has a solid top 10 state ranking. If Player X faces Player Y, who is not as good naturally but is 13 and a half years old and has a top 30 ranking in the state, it will be not surprising that Player Y will outsmart Player X. For the younger player to compete or have a chance to win, he will have to think and come up with a better strategy.

Thinking is required.

Players and coaches both must understand this. Regardless of the individual and their learning style, players must receive simple, precise, and novel information for the brain to assimilate and execute it.

Simple doesn't mean only 1 thing at the time. As I mentioned in the beginning of the book, you can give several instructions to little kids and they can absorb and execute. It just has to be clear for them to understand.

The more this is practiced, the faster it becomes a habit. Mental habits are developed in the exact same way as technical or physical habits.

There are specific mental drills you can practice on the court while hitting that can help you develop those skills.

For example with my advanced players I have a drill that when they are playing points I asked both players to say out loud when the ball is bouncing on their side of the court the side they will be hitting towards. LEFT! If they are hitting to their opponents backhand and RIGHT! When they are hitting to the forehand. They have to do it every time the ball bounces. This allows them to practice focusing because they are listening to the opponents shot selection, and then they have to practice decision making and focusing again because they have to say out loud where they will hit and then they have to actually execute what they said they will do.

It may sound complicated but it is very easy and you can see how much the players start to concentrate and it is easier for them to control shots, because they KNOW what they want. **They have a clear purpose**.

The moment, they hesitate and decide late what to say, the usually make a mistake or hit a defensive neutral shot that the opponent takes advantage of.

This has a complete and direct relation with the Power of Intention. If the intention is not clear, the chances of achieving that goal decrease dramatically.

"The Law of Intention and Desire – This Law is based on the fact that energy and information exist everywhere in nature. The quality of Intention on the object of attention will orchestrate an infinity of space-time events to bring about the outcome intended. Intention lays the groundwork for the effortless, spontaneous, frictionless flow of pure potentiality." – **Deepak Chopra**

Source: https://www.slideshare.net/Duklida/spiritual-laws

The quality of Intention on the object of attention…..To me this is the level of focus you need to decide WHERE to hit the TENNIS BALL.

Intention = *Where to hit*
Object of attention = *Tennis Ball*

This also applies to schools, businesses and so forth. The Intention can potentially be "help kids develop their creativity" or it can be "providing the best home-made tasting burgers to your customers"

The Intention has to be very clear.

Also a simple way of training can be to help players memorize what to do in specific situations and when training. They have to say out loud the shot selection they are making before hitting the shot after they have identify what is coming from the other side and I already explained that in a previous chapter.

You can also ask your players to do the same during competition but they have to do it with their inner-talk.

If it's a technical CHANGE, here I have few examples:

1) Ask the player to repeat specific words during the action and make sure the players actually does it. For example if a player is hitting balls to the net, you can tell him to say before during and after the shot:
   a. Open the face of the racket (**Open**)
   b. Spin it over the net (**Spin Up**)
   c. Extend the arm (**Extend**)
   d. Follow Through (**Finish**)

The player will have to repeat and DO what you expect over and over again in his head.

Open, Spin Up, Extend, Finish … Open, Spin Up, Extend, Finish … Open, Spin Up, Extend, Finish … over and over again until it becomes a habit and you accomplished what you wanted.

If it's a Basic Tactical Change…

2) If someone hits a high ball to my backhand, my player should:
   a. Move forward, and slices it down to opponents backhand
   b. Must repeat the above phrase abbreviated before the ball bounces on his court
   c. The player may abbreviate the phrase with: **Move Forward, Slice down.**
   The player will have to repeat and DO what you expect over and over again in his head.

3) If someone hits a floating shot to the middle, the player:
   a. Moves quickly to the left to hit an inside out forehand
   b. Must repeat the above phrase before the ball bounces on his court.
   c. Can abbreviate the phrase with: **That's a Forehand to his Backhand.**

You can see how you can create many scenarios to train the mind.

CHAPTER

Successful Minds!

> "IF YOU CAN CONCEIVE IT AND BELIEVE IT, YOU CAN ACHIEVE IT." - **Napoleon Hill**

Sources: Think and Grow Rich – Napoleon Hill http://www.success.com/article/rich-man-poor-man

Here is the secret to your success in tennis. Your words and thoughts form your beliefs. Your beliefs create your reality.

As Napoleon Hill said, "If you can conceive it and believe it, you can achieve it."

People in any walk of life, including the world-class tennis players, are successful because they believed they could be ranked at the top. They thought they could win, **they spoke** of achieving a goal, they believed they could do it.

> **"The Word was made Flesh, and dwelt among us." – John 1: 14 KJV**

Source: https://www.biblegateway.com/passage/?search=John+1%3A1 4&version=KJV

Two well-known books are THINK AND GROW RICH by Napoleon Hill and THE SECRET, by Rhonda Byrnes.

These books are among hundreds if not thousands of books that have changed the world. Both authors examined and analyzed the most successful people of their times.

In 1908 at the urging of Andrew Carnegie, Napoleon Hill began a study of more than five hundred of the most influential inventors and multimillionaires. For over twenty years, he assessed the traits that lead to personal success.

Rhonda Byrne studied how belief creates reality, researching the concept thousands of years back. She interviewed some seventy teachers for the movie, sharing what they know about how the mind works for success. They know everything comes from an idea, a concept, a purpose, a belief. They know that when you have a specific idea that is very clear in your head, you are obsessed about accomplishing that idea, you give something in return in the process, you believe you can do it, and you have a plan to do it, then magic happens.

I call this FAITH.

If most successful people know these rules, what we can call natural laws, why in the world don't we follow their advice in the tennis industry?

We can look to characters from the Bible, scientists, philosophers, successful business people, high-performance athletes, Olympians, great professors, and so on. They all knew that positive thoughts and words create positive actions, and these lead to positive results.

Here are practical examples that apply to a tennis player--or any person or situation, for that matter.

Think and Grow Fit

> DO NOT CONFORM TO THE MATTER OF THIS WORLD, BUT BE TRANSFORMED BY THE RENEWING OF YOUR MIND.
> - **Romans 12:2 NIV**

Player "J"

We had a player that started playing tennis around the age of 6. This little kid was so passionate about the sport and her work ethic at that early age was phenomenal. She didn't move as fast as other players but I remember telling her that she had great potential to play advanced tennis if she kept her passion and if she dedicate herself to tennis for at least 5 more years. She retained information so quickly when it came to technical directions and she improved faster than most kids her age.

After about 3 years, she had some loses in a couple of tournaments against kids that were not "supposed" to win against her. I remember the father telling me that his daughter was probably not built to be a tennis player because her footwork and body frame was not there and also because no one played tennis in his family. She didn't have the "pedigree" because her family had baseball players.

Slowly but surely this kid started training not as good as before and she started losing her passion. The parents discourage this kid without even noticing what they were doing. They were afraid of her not reaching her own expectations and they decided that she should stop training after about 3.5 years. I've seen the kid now. She is a teenager and her athletic talent is amazing. She has developed and I think and I'm sure she could have played amazingly but the parents decided to communicate to her negatively and didn't believe in her. Her commitment changed, she got discourage, she stopped playing... The Word became Flesh...

A tennis player can settle for poor performance because he has a certain physique; that's how he came to this world. His genetics and nature "dictate" his body type. His parents, coaches, and friends have always told him he is not very fast or strong because he was born like that. And he buys it. The player can believe this and resign himself to the way his body performs and the way he looks.

Consider also those who have been told they are not athletic enough or smart enough in school to be high-performance athletes or successful in other areas because they were not that good, or they were not interested in mathematics, or they didn't excel in chemistry, or whatever.

I can assure you there are thousands of examples of this mediocre mentality. I will remind you of some.

- **Walt Disney**: Disney was fired from the KANSAS CITY STAR in 1919 because his editor said he "lacked imagination and had no good ideas."
- **Elvis Presley**: After a performance at Nashville's Grand Ole Opry, the concert hall manager told Elvis that he was better off going back to Memphis and driving trucks.

Oprah Winfrey: Oprah was fired from her first job as a co-anchor on Baltimore's WJZ-TV, reportedly because she was "unfit for television news."

- **Brian Acton**: The WhatsApp co-founder was rejected by Facebook for a job in 2009. Five years later, he sold his startup to Facebook for $19 billion.

Source: https://www.vogue.com/article/oprah-winfrey-5-things-you-didnt-know

Michael Jordan, Albert Einstein, Thomas Edison, Stephen King, Benjamin Franklin, and countless successful people experienced situations that looked like failure, but their beliefs allowed them to reach their goals.

The Successful Way

Our tennis player with the "poor" physique can make a conscious decision to improve his body and fitness. The decision can come based on his/her goals, or because of vanity, or because he knows that the stronger the body, the stronger the mind, or because he has a coach who believes he can improve his body dramatically, and that makes the player also believe he can change.

It doesn't really matter where the decision comes from, but it starts with a change of mind. They choose to improve physically; therefore, they will make decisions to eat better, work extra hours, lift weights, hire a fitness coach, read about the body and so on.

The player's initial decision to improve his body and fitness leads to a change of mentality, the change of thoughts, a renewal of the mind--and that change will bring results reflected in his body. He will lose body fat and improve muscle volume; he will get quicker footwork, and he will get stronger and faster.

The Power of Self Talk

A professional player hires a tennis coach after a lunch meeting in which the coach was brutally honest with the player. "Your second serve is awful," he told her, "because you don't know how to toss the ball properly, and that breaks the entire structure of your serve. You can't create margins or enough spin, and that translates to a lack of confidence and lots of mistakes."

She believes her serve is her weakness. She had been told that since she started playing when she was nine. She appreciates the honesty. Her former coach had told her that her serve was bad because she was not consistent and got nervous. She wants a fresh perspective from a new coach.

So, the new coach starts working on the toss. They train hard on that toss, and she feels it is getting better but is not as accurate and consistent as they would like.

Once she gets better at the toss, after they've used slow motion video to make corrections, they realize the spin is still not good enough, and she has to work on that too. And the story goes on.

After "fixing" the problem, she goes into a big tournament and during the first rounds she does very well against lower ranked players. But in the quarterfinals, she faces a higher ranked player, and her serve falls apart.

Why did that happen?

If you are following me, you will realize that the problem showed up again because her mentality changed a little bit but not completely. She thought she was getting better because she was working the technical part of the serve. However, her subconscious mind was not being trained consistently in order to change the negative concept she had about her serve.

So, now some of you will say, "But how can she say that her serve is good now and believe it, if is not true? She can't lie to herself!"

You are right. She can't just change her mind like that and believe her serve is amazing. The coach also would never be able to make the corrections and improve her serve, because he also believed her serve was awful in the first place. They both started with the incorrect state of mind or mentality, as Einstein said in the quote above.

In order to change the problem of the bad serve, the coach and the player have to change their mentality.

Remember: She has been told her serve was bad since she was nine years old. Do you think her subconscious has been trained properly?

No way.

The Successful Way

It is going to sound very simple, but the correct approach from the player—and reinforced by her new coach--should have been something like this: "I want my serve to be as good as my ground strokes, so I will make some modifications to reach that goal."

Also, every time she was training her serve she could have used her inner talk to say something like: "I'm practicing my toss and my serve will keep improving and I trust it will respond under pressure moments."

Again, it sounds easy and obvious, but most people do not think that way. She has to work on her toss. Ideally, while practicing it, she should silently repeat to herself every time she is tossing the ball something like this: "I am having a perfect toss, and this will make my serve an amazing shot!"

By doing this, she is training her subconscious mind, she is shaping her thoughts, and she is also changing her mentality.

Some Olympians already train like this. They repeat positive phrases and comments about themselves. We need to start this when our players are very young and never stop the process.

It's all about changing our minds.

Consider the wisdom of Tony Robbins., who has changed thousands of lives by teaching similar concepts: "If you do what you've always done, you'll get what you've always gotten."

If at First You Don't Succeed…

WHETHER YOU THINK YOU CAN, OR THINK YOU CAN'T, YOU ARE RIGHT. – **Henry Ford**

If you are a coach, a parent, or player, you probably have experienced the scenario of not being able to win against a player who is not even close to your technical and physical level.

It's the typical story that keeps repeating itself. You have a better serve or a better forehand, you are more athletic, you have better returns, volleys and even a better hand, but every time you face that player, you have issues because he is extremely consistent and is willing to stay on the court for hours. So, you keep telling yourself, your coach and/or your parents, that you can't win against him. "It's impossible! He is a nightmare! I can't stay there pushing balls all day!!"

Of course you lose to him. And in the next round a friend who plays at your level wins easily against him. You do not comprehend how in the world he is able to do it--and with such ease. The "nightmare" player performs better against you, but when he faces someone else, he stinks!

You ask the winner how he did it, and he tells you, "You hit to the backhand and attack to the net. It's super easy."

But you don't believe your friend because you have tried that before against the nightmare player in other matches. And every time you go to the net, he passes you like a racecar passes a school bus, or he hits super high lobs that make you go back to the baseline.

Again, if you are following me, you will know by now that the scenario happens to you because that's exactly what you believe will happen.

There is a phrase that says:
"What you fear, you draw near."

It also applies also in the typical scenario of 5-5 (30/30): You are serving, and obviously, you think you don't want to double fault. Do you know what happens when you don't want to double fault? Yes, you guessed right. You double fault. It's a mentality problem. It applies to business, even personal relationships.

Some people keep choosing partners that are abusive, lazy, etc. They keep telling their friends and family, "I always have bad luck in picking a partner. I always choose the lazy ones and disrespectful ones. I don't want to choose incorrectly again!"

You know what happens, right?

Exactly.

The Successful Way

The simple way to change this is by changing your mentality. The result may not come immediately. Instead of telling everyone you can't win against the nightmare pusher or counter-attacker, you have to think:

Next time I face him, I will move him, and when he gives me a chance, I will attack to the net by hitting to his backhand, no matter if he passes me or not. If I execute this every time, I will have a better chance to win. Sooner or later I will get him!"

Belief Creates Reality

> "THE MIND IS EVERYTHING. WHAT YOU THINK, YOU BECOME." – Buddha

I already talked about this but a kid born in a family with no high-performance athletic pedigree and a poor economic environment may hear that he will never achieve success in tennis because he doesn't have the right genetics, the family can't afford the training, and in their country, they do not support athletes.

Some outstanding kids have the strength to ignore what they hear and create their opportunities by training hard and believing in their dreams.

Take the example of Jefferson Perez, the Olympic medalist from my country, Ecuador, and the only man in history to win the 20km walk world title three years in a row.

Perez was born into poverty. As a child, Perez helped support his family by shining shoes. "My only interest then was to help my family financially," he said in an interview during his Documentary (Los Zapatitos de Oro) "We were very poor and my intention was to get a job as soon as possible to offer support.

"I was exposed to everything in my youth: crime, drugs, you name it," Perez said. "But I guess I was signed for something different, and that kept me away from all those temptations that usually present themselves to young kids."

Source: https://www.youtube.com/watch?v=WCmSXJVjyGg Jefferson Perez Documentary – Los Zapatitos de Oro /

His nutrition was inadequate even while he was training for the Olympics because he used the nutrition/diet allowance from the Federation and sponsors to build a little house for his mother. He told his coaches he was following a specific diet, while he was barely eating. But he BELIEVED he could win the Olympics, even though he was malnourished.

Interesting? For sure. We could write a book about him and his strong mentality. He was able to face obstacles his entire life because he never felt like a victim. He created his journey with faith and hard work. I hope one day I have the privilege to meet such an outstanding human being.

But what if the kid is average and follows their parents' mentality, as most kids would do? Then he would become a mid-level player/athlete/human being.

I recently spoke to a parent who is new to the sport of tennis. He has been involved in baseball and American football. He was actually a great quarterback and played at a level in college. He said he heard from another tennis parent that if your kid is not winning against high-ranked eighteen-year-olds by the time they are thirteen or fourteen, they have no chance to make it to professional levels in the sport of tennis. I'm not here to judge anyone, but I prefer to have a positive mentality, attitude and faith that dreams can come true.

Don't get me wrong. I know we also have to be realistic, and if your kid is fourteen and is just learning to play tennis, the chances of going pro decrease a lot.

But remember: the point of playing tennis and competing is not making it to pro level. The purpose of playing tennis or any other sport is the pursuit of personal excellence: improving, discipline, learning about yourself, etc. That's a chapter we will cover later.

Some parents or coaches tell their kids:

- You are not good under pressure
- You always mess up things
- You don't listen to me

You know what the kid ends up believing? Exactly!
What they think, they become.

They believe those words, and then what? How in the world are they going to erase all those negative comments and believe they are great? They need some wise guidance and understanding.

Can you see what we are printing in the subconscious of our young players and athletes?

"Everybody is a genius. But if you judge a fish by its ability to climb a tree, it will live its entire life believing that it is stupid" - **Unknown**

We have to HELP THEM NOW.

We, coaches make mistakes every single day. We tell kids they don't know how to move, or that they are slow, or that they choke in complicated moments. I include myself because I continue to make mistakes. But when you are aware of mistakes, you are on the path of change and improvement. Just like when you are inside the court and you are aware of your mistakes and decide to make changes. It is something we must do at all times.

The tennis industry must start changing for good. We have to build our players in the same way they have to build points. But our mindset must change, and for that to happen, we have to be aware. We will cover that very important word and concept later in a different chapter.

I want to clarify that by this I'm not saying kids or players do not have to work hard and dedicate themselves to reach high levels. It's important not to mix both concepts. If you read chapter 1, you know for a fact that all players MUST go through level 2 which is be a builder and hard worker in order to reach level 3 which is The Zone or autopilot levels.

The Successful Way and Actual Fact

If you are a big tennis fan, coach, or player, you probably have seen on YouTube the first interview of Novak Djokovic when he was only six or seven years old. I do not speak Serbian, but if the person who translated the video is correct, you can see how Novak was thinking at an early age. He says that tennis is his duty and that his goal is to be number one.

Source: **https://www.youtube.com/watch?v=tdOS0zCsJsg**

When he said that, their parents could have stopped him and told him to stop dreaming, but what happened?

I'm assuming his family and environment believed in him and supported him in his dream. And guess what happened? Djokovic became what he was focusing or thinking about. Remember Buddha's quote? Let me remind you again so you don't have to turn the page back.

> *The mind is everything. What you think, you become.* – **Buddha**

As tennis coaches, players, or parents, we have to be aware and conscious on a daily basis about our thoughts and words because those will create our reality and the reality of people around us.

This brings us to the next chapter that will help you realize how your level of Mental Awareness can help you.

> YOU CAN'T PUT A LIMIT ON ANYTHING. THE MORE YOU DREAM, THE FARTHER YOU GET. – **Michael Phelps**

5

We are Energy. Energy Transforms. Thoughts and Words Create.

> *"Learn how to see. Realize that everything connects to everything else." - **Leonardo Da Vinci***

Since you already know and understand the three mental levels from chapter 1, it's time to talk about quantum physics.

QUANTUM PHYSICS

Here is the "expert definition" of it: Quantum theory is the theoretical basis of modern physics that explains the nature and behavior of matter and energy on the atomic and subatomic level. The nature and behavior of matter and energy at that level is sometimes referred to as quantum physics and quantum mechanics.

You may be wondering what quantum physics has to do with tennis. Good question! I ask you to be patient and read this chapter, because if you get the proven theory behind this information, you will be amazed.

If you are a bit familiar with physics or quantum mechanics, you know that everything is energy, including your thoughts. You probably also know that energy transforms constantly and that human beings are considered to be both energy and matter due to us having a soul/spirit and a physical body as well.

Also, if you are part of the blessed population that has been educated and guided through a school or university, you probably have heard the expression: mind over matter.

The phrase "mind over matter" first appeared in 1863 in THE GEOLOGICAL EVIDENCE OF THE ANTIQUITY OF MAN by Sir Charles Lyell (1797–1875) and was first used to refer to the increasing status and evolutionary growth of the minds of animals and man throughout Earth's history. In short, it refers to the power of the mind to control and influence the body and the physical world.

Most people know this concept, but they are not truly aware of its meaning and the impact it can have in our lives and the way we rationalize or think on a daily basis.

It's a very simple concept that has been proven over and over again. It also has been recognized not only by physicists but by the majority of educated people in different professional fields.

Some people believe quantum physics is a modern concept, however, the initial discoveries were made in the early 1900s.

Human Thought Determines Reality

> Positive Thoughts = **FAITH**
> Negative Thoughts = **FEAR**
> **FEAR** = Fall Evidence Appearing **R**eal

The following information will help you understand how your thinking can improve your tennis game – and your life.

"One of the key principles of quantum physics is that our thoughts determine reality. Early in the 1900s they proved this with an experiment called the double slit experiment. They found that the determining factor of the behavior of energy ('particles') at the quantum level is the awareness of the observer.

"For example: electrons under the same conditions would sometimes act like particles, and then at other times they would switch to acting like waves (formless energy), because it was completely dependent on what the observer expected was going to happen. Whatever the observer believed would occur is what the quantum field did." - Brandon West for "Waking Times" [2]

Deepak Chopra, the well-known writer and spiritual coach who has written more than 50 books and has several New York Times best sellers, mentions the concept of particles and waves in his book *The Spontaneous fulfillment of Desire* and tells us the concept is known as the **Heisenberg Uncertainty Principle** and this concept "it's one of the fundamental building blocks of modern physics" – Deepak Chopra (The Spontaneous Fulfillment of Desire)

If electrons can change from particles to waves depending on the belief of the observer and what he expects, then it makes sense that we can use this information in tennis. Let's consider a few examples.

Example 1: Junior player chokes in the presence of parents or coach

Why do some junior players behave differently, depending on if the coach is watching or the parents are watching?

Imagine Player "Z" playing in a semifinals match, serving, and the score is 5-6 (30/30) on the third set. He is trying to hold serve and he misses an easy approach shot. Then the score is (30/40) match points against him, and he double faults.

---

[2] http://www.wakingtimes.com/2014/04/16/proof-human-body-projection-consciousness/

If the parents witnessed the match, they probably asked him why he choked at (30/30) and why he double faulted at the end. Do you think the kid could be thinking about that speech the next time he is in that situation with his parents? Probably, yes.

Do you think the observers/parents will be afraid of the same thing happening again and may have a negative expectation the next time the kid is in that situation? You are right again. Yes.

On the other hand, Player "Z's" coach has seen the kid in that type of pressure situation a lot of times during training and tournaments. He knows the player can overcome it, and his expectations are completely different. He is excited at (30-30) watching his player, and he tells him, "LET'S GO, MACHINE! You can do this!"

Do you think the coach's (the observer) belief and expectations could affect more positively Player Z's outcome and the result of the match?

Probably yes!

Even if the kid doesn't perform as expected, the observer can have a huge impact on the player (the particle.) After missing those two points, the coach can say, "Player 'Z' you missed the approach and double faulted, but you did what you had to because you attacked the short ball and you accelerated both serves with no fear. Great job! Next time you will get him!"

Keep in mind that this is only an example that can apply in different ways. Perhaps the coach criticizes a lot and the parents are more positive "observers" of Player "Z".

Example 2: "Pro player improves his strategy and attacking style with new coach"

Pro player "Y" has very solid groundstrokes and likes to battle from the baseline for hours. His current coach (the observer) tells her constantly that she is not a volley player, her backhand volley is not solid, and the best game for her is to stay back and control her opponents with her powerful groundstrokes. He says she is talented physically, and she can stay there longer than most female players.

If this is the situation, player "Y" (the particle) will believe those words, and when she has the chance to go to the net, she may not commit because she lacks confidence on her volleys.

But if the observer is a different coach whose philosophy is to be more strategic with spaces and he likes his players moving forward and not extending matches, that coach can see player "Y" and have completely different expectations of her. He can think she has to improve her backhand volley, and once she is better at it, she will be a more complete player. They will work together on that specific thing.

The expectation of the coach (observer) impacts the result of the player (particle). This happens every day on the tennis courts, but few people are aware of the quantum changes taking place right in front of their eyes. It is magical.

The theory that particles change behavior based on the expectations of the observer apply to everything.

For example, sometimes a student in school behaves better with one teacher than with others because that teacher has higher expectations or a different perspective about the kid.

Consider a guy who sees his girlfriend as boring. Perhaps his expectations are incorrect, so he breaks up with her. A new boyfriend may see her as the coolest girlfriend because he invites her to different events, and she is always ready and happy to go.

Even children in the same family may see each other differently. One sibling may think the parents are mean to him because they are too strict. But the other sibling may think the parents are great because they give them structure and values.

Get it? It is everywhere and it happens all the time. Now you can understand the physics behind Wayne Dyer's maxim: Change the way you look at things, and the things you look at change. We will talk more about Wayne Dyer's quote later in the book.

We have the chance to be alchemists every day and color our lives exactly the shade we choose.

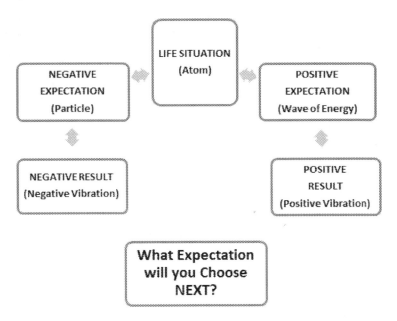

JOSÉ ANTONIO CASARES-FALCONI

6

Mind Over Matter in Tennis

"Create the highest, grandest vision possible for your life, because you become what you believe." – Oprah Winfrey.

THE BIOLOGY OF BELIEVE IN TENNIS

After more than thirty years of studying human cells and their behavior, Bruce H. Lipton, Ph.D., concluded that the body works differently than we originally thought. Thousands of studies showed him that genes and DNA do not control our biology; instead DNA is controlled by signals outside the cell, including energetic messages emanating from our positive and negative thoughts. Lipton wrote a book called THE BIOLOGY OF BELIEF, in which he proposes that all the cells of the human body are affected by these thoughts.

I believe Dr. Lipton also discovered that cells behave differently based on the environment in which they are located.

"This profoundly hopeful synthesis of the latest and best research in cell biology and quantum physics is being hailed as a major breakthrough, showing that our bodies can be changed as we retrain our thinking." -Dr. Bruce Lipton Ph.D. (The Biology of Believe).

This may sound absurd to some people, but if you analyze this concept and think it through, you will see that makes a lot of sense.

I watched a conference in which Dr. Lipton explained how they chose twenty or thirty people with knee issues and told them they would receive surgery to correct the problem. They divided them into two groups. They performed corrective surgery on the members of one group, recording the procedures in a video. Members of the second group experienced only a small incision in the knee. They were shown a video recording of the complete corrective procedure later.

Do you know what happened? Both groups recovered successfully from their knee issues, even though half of them didn't have surgery. This, of course, is called the "placebo effect."

I'm sure you have heard about the placebo effect, the phenomenon that a patient's symptoms can be alleviated by an otherwise ineffective treatment if the individual believes it will work.

For me this concept is related to my Christian faith: what you believe is what is.

You can find the concept of the placebo effect used in tennis academies and other tennis environments. Some academies and coaches will preach about a specific thing that will make players improve and, sure enough, the students will improve.

For example, a player with solid technical fundamentals can go through a stroke video analysis, and the coach may "discover" his toss and shoulders on the serve are not as aligned as the coach would like. They make the "correction," and in the first attempt, the player serves up the line, and it works perfectly. When this happens, the player BELIEVES in the change, so he trusts the coach and will continue to practice the toss and shoulder turn to satisfy the coach's eye and point of view. After weeks or months of working in that specific change, the player will be serving much better and will be thankful about the change he made with the toss and shoulder turn.

Now, the coach records another video to see the correction implemented. But – and I kid you not – most of the time, the toss and shoulder turn HAS NOT CHANGED AT ALL. Keep in mind the player is serving better.

How in the world do you explain this? Only that the player BELIEVED they implemented the correction. It's crazy, but it happens all the time.

The biology of belief applies to negative things also, as we have already discussed. If you tell your student, player, or child that they are not good listeners, they will BELIEVE you. So, do not be surprised if they listen even less. What you believe is what is. Faith equals belief and vice versa.

> *"Do you believe in miracles?" – Al Michaels*

I've taught some of my older students how powerful the mind can be with a simple example.

When someone has an "eating disorder," he/she may see herself in the mirror as overweight. Even though her family and friends see how skinny he really is, he will see himself as gigantic in the mirror. His mind believes he is big, and that's what the eyes also see. Can you imagine how powerful the mind is that it can distort the perception of the eyes and make us see things that are not physically real?

Let me repeat that. *The mind can distort the perception of the eyes and make us see things that are not physically real.*

Now, think about the environment where a player spends his time every day, and the people around him. It can be his home, his team, his academy, family, school, friends and so forth. All these can impact negatively or positively a tennis player.

Motivational speaker Jim Rohn said that we are the average of the five people we spend the most time with. Dr. Lipton has verified this idea in the body.

Dr. Lipton discussed an experiment with a person who suffered from muscular dysfunction. When he studied the affected cells in the patient's environment, the cells continued to degenerate. When Dr. Lipton studied the cells away from the patient's environment, the cells began to heal and develop appropriately.

This may also sound a bit crazy, but think about it. When you analyze normal life situations, you know that when someone hangs around the wrong crowd, they become similar to that group of people.

Have you ever witnessed, for example, an athlete who should not be tall or strong because the parents are small and short? But he started training at an early age, and somehow, he grew tall and strong? How do you explain this?

An example is Michael Jordan. Probably the greatest basketball player of all time, Jordan came from a family that was not genetically tall enough to create a potential NBA player.

Michael Jordan's dad was 5'9" and his mom was 5'5".

Another good example is Jeremy Lee. He is an Asian American NBA Player and both of his parents stand at 5'6"

If Dr. Lipton is right, environment influences outcomes.
Of course, the way a kid and his parents think has an equally strong influence, especially if the parents never limited him by saying "Don't play basketball because you will be too short for that sport." Maybe the parents supported the kid and told him that if he wants to pursuit that sport, go for it.

CHANGE YOUR POINT OF VIEW

> "The things you look at CHANGE, when you CHANGE the way you look at things." – Wayne Dyer

Dr. Bruce Lipton's theory of environmental influence is related to quantum physics and to a concept stressed by the highly respected spiritual teacher Dr. Wayne Dyer, whom I mentioned earlier.

"Change the way you look at things, and the things you look at change," Dyer said. "This is just not a clever play on words. It is actually a very scientific thing."

I can assure you that, if you start experimenting with this in tennis, you will prove the point. Try it.

If you are a coach with a player who, in your point of view, doesn't move that well, change the way you look at him. Tell him he has all the potential he needs to be a great mover. Tell him every day how much his footwork has improved. You will see that almost instantly he will start moving better, and if you continue to do it, he will continue to improve. When you change the concept you had of him, you will change your communication with him, and therefore, the results will change.

I've done many experiments that prove this concept.

I have a sixteen-year-old player who started playing with me when she was only nine. She is passionate about the sport and as disciplined as you would wish a player to be. But, when we did any type of drill when she was younger than 11, she would get tense, and you could see the tension even in her facial expressions. You may think it was just a normal reaction for a beginning player, but in her case, it was extreme.

When I saw she was tensing so much, I started experimenting with different methods.

I made her chew gum, whistle, sing, and so forth while she was hitting the ball during practices. All these methods work during drills, and she was getting better, but when she competed and could not chew gum or sing, she would tense up again, and this would affect her strokes and movement. She would run to the ball tense, and that would make her get to the ball late, and her technique would break structurally.

I didn't know what to do at this point, so I asked her to write a list of all her fears. She brought me a list of twenty-two fears, from getting sick to not being able to improve.

I asked her to review the list with her parents so they could explain to her that everything was going to be okay. I also reviewed the list with her to make sure she understood that most of her fears were non-existent; they were illusions.

She improved a lot, but the improvement was only temporary. I continued to believe that she had tendencies of tensing in stressful situations, and my communication with her was the same.

Then I realized that the way I looked at her tendency to tense was the same. No wonder I kept getting the same "tensing" results when she was competing during training.

I decided to change my point of view about her and communicate differently. I decided to believe that she could be the most fluid and relaxed player we had, based on her discipline, commitment, and passion for the sport. She always followed everything I said, so I decided not just to change my point of view about her. I started telling her that she was looking so relaxed and becoming the most fluid player in the academy.

You know what happened?

Yes, you are right. She changed completely, and now she is so fluid, and seeing her hit every shot is a great experience.

For her to change, I had to change the way I looked at her. And now she is outstanding because her challenge has become her passion.

I started working with another player when she was eight years old. She was smart and consistent. She made her opponents move from side to side and waited until the right time to be aggressive. When she started growing and learning to accelerate, she picked up some cross concepts in her environment. She began to think that tennis was about accelerating and taking control of the opponent with force and speed. This concept may be followed by lots of coaches and schools, but I disagree. Tennis is a sport of consistency, feeling and timing and controlling yourself, not the opponent.

Consistency is the foundation for everything. It is the foundation of a point. Without consistency, you cannot attack and control the point. I'm sure you'll agree that even when you attack you have to be consistent.

She started making many mistakes during practices and especially during competition. She had a nice technique that would allow her to have control and power, but she was not clicking during competition, and the unforced errors kept limiting her from improving as we would have liked. This naturally consistent player changed, I believe, because she changed how she thought of herself and her game.

Other people kept stressing acceleration and control of the point, and her mistakes continued. No wonder: if you are a kid, this could be confusing if the concept of margins of error is not clear in your head.

Then I made a mistake and joined the way other people thought about her. I started telling her not to make too many mistakes and that she was not consistent. Unfortunately, she believed us. She believed she was not consistent.

We struggled with this concept for two years until I decided to remind her how consistent and patient she was when she was younger. I started telling her that she is consistent and that she has always been consistent, and that with some new drills she will be back to normal.

Instead of seeing her as an inconsistent player, I changed my point of view about her, and I gave her another definition as a player. I believe she is consistent because that's how she was since she was eight years old, and I communicate that with her. The results are starting to show, and it is like magic.

We are doing exercises during morning practices that force us to hit 120 balls without missing, while changing patterns and directions. Sure, she made some mistakes in the beginning, but after twenty minutes, we got in the zone, and she proved she was able to focus and be as consistent as she wanted. We did more than seven exercises with the same conditions: 120 shots between both without missing any shots, changing patterns and directions, with different themes, and she did phenomenally.

Remember: when you change the way you look at things, the things you looked at change.
Consider these simple and clear examples:
General way: She is not a consistent player.
Changed way: I believe she will be consistent with some practice and patience from me.

General way: He is a smoker, and he is addicted to it.
Changed way: If other people have quit smoking, I'm positive he can quit also.

General way: She has a terrible point of contact; therefore, her spin is inconsistent.
Changed way: She keeps working on her point of contact. With time, she will spin the ball very well.

General way: When I'm giving the class, most students are not paying attention.
Changed way: All my students are energetic and active, so I will find an active way to teach them.

General way: My husband works too many hours, and we don't spend lots of time together.
Changed way: I'm so blessed because my husband has a secure job that allows us to pay for our needs.

General way: The food at this restaurant is terrible, and they better give me my money back.
Changed way: I'm sure the chef is doing his best. They are extremely busy today. I will talk to them nicely.

General way: My student is so inconsistent, and he never gets my point.
Changed way: My student's potential is unlimited; I will help him become a wall.

General way: My student always makes bad decisions on the court.
Changed way: My student is still learning, and with time he will be a great decision maker.

General Way: My employees are so inefficient!
Changed Way: I will train and guide my employees until they reach my level of expertise.

When you change the way you look at things, the things you look at will change. Try it and witness Magical things!

EVERY EXTERNAL CHANGE COMES FROM AN INTERNAL CHANGE

I believe it is important to mention again the quote below…

> *When we are no longer able to change a situation, we are challenged to change ourselves. – Victor E. Frankl*

Max Planck was given the Noble Price in Physics for his work on the atom. Planck is considered one of the greatest scientific minds ever. Wayne Dyer said that Planck is a physicist, so he needed hard data and the means to measure and calculate results. Physicists don't believe in random spiritual theories.

Dyer said that while Planck accepted the Nobel Prize in Physics, he alluded to a consciousness in the universe:

"As a man who has devoted his whole life to the most clear-headed science, to the study of matter, I can tell you, as the result of my research about atoms this much; there is no matter as such. All matter originates and exists only by virtue of a force which brings the particle of an atom to vibration and holds this most minute solar system of the atom together. We MUST assume behind this force the existence of a conscious and intelligent mind. This mind is the matrix of all matter."

Now, if you understand Planck, you can assume different things. They can be related with religion, physics, biology, even tennis, and so forth.

However, it is clear he says THE MIND IS THE MATRIX OF ALL MATTER. Therefore, we could agree with the well-known concept: MIND OVER MATTER.

The mind-over-matter concept is the power of the mind to control and influence the body and the physical world.

For example: "A human being walking over hot coals."

It is the use of willpower to overcome physical problems.

It is used to describe a situation in which someone is able to control a physical condition, problem, etc., by using the mind. "His ability to keep going even when he is tired is a simple question of mind over matter."

Marathon runners speak ominously about a sudden wave of fatigue that sets in at about twenty miles into the twenty-six-mile race. They call this "hitting the wall." At this point, they say, the race is (only) half over.

In endurance sports such as cycling and running, hitting the wall is a condition of sudden fatigue and loss of energy which is caused by the depletion of glycogen stores in the liver and muscles.

If you know any runners, they may have told you that the best way of pushing through this wall is by being mentally strong and not accepting the physical deterioration that the body is experiencing during those last miles. They will tell you their inner speech and internal dialogue has to be positive, otherwise you can put fthe entire race in jeopardy and stop right before the finish line. When they hit this wall, runners feel physical pain everywhere, and if they use the mind incorrectly, the race will be over for them.

I believe in tennis we face this wall all the time, and not only physically. I believe we face this wall in different situations during every match we play. The match will test you physically, emotionally, mentally, and tactically. The player who surrenders mentally first probably is the one who will lose. However, with right use of the mind, you can control the other factors.

In tennis, the mental battle sometimes starts days before, when you see the draw and study your opponent. It continues when you are visualizing the match, when you see the opponents' eyes, when you meet them, during the first point, after executing a second serve and the opponent attacks it, when realizing your game plan is not working or you cannot execute it.

Club players and junior players sometimes surrender to this wall before the match has even started or during the initial games of the first set. If you are a coach or a parent, you know exactly what I'm talking about.

Sometimes they wake up during the second set when it is a bit late, and they have to row against the current. Sometimes this happens when they are warming up and the other player "impresses" the opponent by hitting a hard shot. I believe this also happens when "rookies" enter the professional environment and start facing highly ranked players. *Out of respect, sometimes they give the match away.*

During professional matches, you can tell sometimes when the momentum changes, the energy changes, and one of the players stops when he has encountered that wall. The top performers face that wall better than average performers. Perhaps it is a natural talent; who knows?

Or they have faced that situation more often and have learned to push through. Maybe their coaches have taught them to anticipate hitting the wall, so they are "more ready."

What if we start working on this with kids at five, six, or seven years old? I'm sure we could have a great impact on every player.

In the same way marathoners expect to hit the wall, all tennis players should be trained prior to facing it. It should be part of daily training, or at least mentioned frequently to prepare players to face the situation with more awareness.

Consider the following mind-over-matter examples that apply to all situations of this great sport.

TECHNICAL application of the mind-over-matter concept:

You want a player to improve his forehand preparation and follow through. To accomplish this technical change, first you would explain to the player what you want. You may show him a video or demonstrate the "correct" motion and compare it with his. After watching the video and your demonstration, the player automatically or subconsciously will visualize those changes before trying to make the correction.

In the second stage, you might ask the player to perform the motion without hitting the ball. At this stage, the player is using his mind to gather information you provide before playing it again in his brain and then making the motion you desire. If you agree with what he has done without the ball, then you would proceed to the next step.

At this point, you feed balls or start rallying with the player to practice executing the new, desired technique. For this to happen, before, during and after hitting, the player must focus and repeat the desired motion time after time without losing focus, to create muscle memory and develop the new biomechanical habit.

I've explained this in detail so you understand that a technical change will not occur without a mental change.

The mind-over-matter concept applies every time we do a technical change. Mental work comes before technical development.

My formula for technical changes is:

Mental and Visual (Keep in mind visual comes from mental)
Mental, Visual, Action
Mental, Action, Mental, Action, Mental, Action. Repeat

RESULT: The new habit or change has been accomplished.

PHYSICAL application of the mind-over-matter concept:

You want your player to develop stronger core muscles. Reflecting on my formula, you first implement the Mental and Visual stage. You talk to your player. You show him videos of pro players or high-performance athletes with very strong core muscles, and offer the exercises they need to work on.

In the second stage, Mental, Visual, Action, you demonstrate the exercises and show the player what you want. You ask the player to repeat the exercises to make sure he is doing them correctly.

In the third stage – Mental, Action, Mental, Action, Mental, Action. Repeat – the player has to repeat, remember the exercises (mental), and then repeat the action of the exercises repeatedly. If the player performs this process repeatedly, they will develop stronger core muscles.

In the fourth stage, your player has a strong core and their strokes are maximized by the power of their physique.

The formula for physical changes would be the same:

Mental and Visual (Keep in mind visual comes from mental)
Mental, Visual, Action
Mental, Action, Mental, Action, Mental, Action. Repeat

RESULT: The new habit or change has been accomplished.
So remember always! Every external change comes from an internal change.

> "Our lives change externally as we change internally." – **Caroline Myss.**

Hal Elrod wrote the best seller THE MIRACLE MORNING: THE NOT-SO-OBVIOUS SECRET GUARANTEED TO TRANSFORM YOUR LIFE.

At age twenty, he was in a car accident that left him in a coma for nearly a week. He said that the first two weeks after the accident are a blur and that he only knows what happened because of stories from his family and friends. Doctors feared he would not be able to walk again. There was even the chance that he would never come out of the coma.

Before the accident, Hal had a mentor who taught him a valuable life lesson. His mentor told him that there is nothing you can do to change the past. He also learned to not be upset about anything for more than three minutes, because it doesn't help. When Hal regained consciousness after two weeks, he applied those principles, and became happy and positive about life. When the doctors saw his positive attitude, they told his parents Hal was not realistic about what the future might bring. They recommended that the parents encourage him to be realistic about his negative physical condition.

When Hal's father asked him why he was being so positive when he might not be able to walk again, Hal told his father that his three minutes to be negative were long over. He chose to stay positive and look forward to what the future had prepared for him. He said that if he was going to need a wheelchair, he decided to be the happiest person in a wheelchair. The parents and doctors respected his attitude about his situation. Guess what happened?

Hal began showing amazing signs of recovery that the doctors couldn't explain. Hal walked out of the hospital in just seven weeks.

My point is that even in terms of health, to change the body, first you must change the mind.

Here is an example of how these internal/external changes apply to tennis:

I have a student who just turned nine years old. He is a great little kid who is becoming passionate about the sport and can be a great player in the future. I'm going to call him CM.

When CM joined our tennis academy, he was only seven, and most of us judged him incorrectly. We complained about him not listening to us. We thought he didn't have discipline, lacked concentration, and was never willing to follow instructions.

The players in our Academy train with all our coaches so they can experience different perspectives and feedback. None of us knew what to do for CM. But my mom did! She suggested I practice what I preach and change MY attitude and approach to CM.

That day, instead of giving him orders and yelling at him, I said to his peers, "Guys, come here! I'm going to do a forehand drill with CM. I want you to watch CM hit his forehands and watch his footwork, because he is doing great. You all can learn from how well he listens and see what an amazing forehand he has. He is hitting his forehand so well that I'm going to call him The Forehand Doctor!"

I wish you could have seen CM's eyes and happy face. It was as if I did some magic trick; he was hypnotized and watching me with pride and very grateful about me actually believing in him.

Unbelievably, when we started the drill, CM indeed started hitting and moving better. Not only that he improved automatically, but now CM ALWAYS listens to me. Always.

So my question to you now is: Who changed first? Did CM change or did I change?

Of course, I changed first, which positively impacted CM. He then changed and improved.

I could have continued to blame CM because he didn't listen and lacked discipline. Instead I decided to look at myself, analyze how I was treating him, and make adjustments to get different results. It is magical. I recommend doing that in any situation, and you will be amazed. It applies not only to tennis but to love relationships, work relationships, business transactions, and so on.

Remember again that every external change comes from an internal change. CM is the external factor and I am the internal factor.

It is not easy to do it all the time, and I continue to make mistakes with my students and in life. Awareness is the first step. Small changes and improvements will affect positively not only your students, family members, friends, and coworkers, but especially yourself.

> "Progress is impossible without change, and those who cannot change their minds cannot change anything." – **George Bernard Shaw**

THE BATTLE AGAINST OURSELVES

You know, of course, that to become good at tennis – or anything – takes discipline, consistency, and effort.

Some say that *if you do what you love, you love what you do;* then it becomes effortless. It is not hard because it's easier to enjoy even the difficult moments.

I believe both concepts are correct, but whether you love what you do or not, there will always be challenges. I'm not talking about external battles-- like facing an opponent with a monster forehand like Rafa Nadal, or an opponent with a rocket-type serve like Karlovic or Isner, or a manager or coach who doesn't treat you as well as you would like. I'm talking about the internal (mental and spiritual) battle you have to face in all external challenges.

I will give you an easy tennis example:

All of our students are different, for obvious reasons. To make the example practical, I will divide the students in two groups, the defenders or patient players and the aggressive or impatient players.

The naturally patient players do not like to take many risks. For those more consistent players, sometimes called "pushers," it is not comfortable to move forward and attack a short ball. Sometimes, even if they are one step away from the service line, instead of hitting an approach shot and moving into the net, they decide to move back and continue the rally from the baseline. They thrive on long rallies, making the opponent hit so many balls that they feel miserable and start making mistake after mistake.

> "If you cannot control your Mind, everything and everyone else will." – **Joe Dispenza**

I tell my students that for a defender player to become more of a complete and balanced player, he or she has to become more aggressive. I think that's easy to see, and it makes sense to most of us.

The battle against themselves comes when they have to do something they do not love to do. In this case, the naturally defensive players will have to push themselves to become more aggressive, move forward, hit easy shots, create approach opportunities, finish points, or take risks.

On the other hand, we have the naturally aggressive players who like to take risks and love to control the point. If they have a chance to hit a short ball, they will try to find a winner shot and experience that addictive feeling of power, control over their destiny and, especially, instant satisfaction.

I also tell my aggressive students that for them to become more complete and balanced players, they need to learn to be more consistent and patient. "Wait for the right opportunity or don't pull the trigger at all." It's a challenge.

The aggressive player's internal battle is to NOT gamble and try to hit a winning shot. This aggressive instinct in many of my students is a gift, but too often, they can't execute it properly, and they miss the shot. The RIGHT decision is to feel that approach, hit with some nice margins, and move into the net to increase the chances of winning the point without risking too much.

I have a funny concept I tell my students to illustrate the inner battle.

Every time they have an easy shot, the aggressive players have an awesome chance to battle against themselves, become better players, and control the shot without risking too much. If they do not control themselves, and instead over-hit an approach and make a mistake, I tell them they just ate a nice, huge, chocolate chip cookie. "**YOU ATE THE COOKIE!**"

I have a sweet tooth, and to stay healthy and control my weight, I need to say "no thanks" when I see a chocolate chip cookie. If every time I see a cookie I eat it, trust me: I will not be a balanced man. I am balanced when I control myself and say, "No thanks, I ate a cookie yesterday." I pass, even if my nature is to have a sweet tooth. If I surrender to the temptation to eat a cookie, I have made a bad decision and have not been able to control myself. I lose the battle against myself.

I also share the concept of asking someone on a date or to dance with you. The aggressive player finds it easier to approach a date and ask for a phone number, but sometimes timing can be very important. If a girl doesn't want a pushy guy, he needs to have patience and wait for the right time to ask.

If you are a defensive player, maybe it's not easy for you to talk to a girl or a boy. So, it may be good to push yourself to get out of your comfort zone, build some courage, and introduce yourself before someone else does it first.

I think you understand my point. Balance and battling against yourself is key.

Whether you are an aggressive or a defensive player, I hope you are not eating cookies all the time.

As a coach or a parent of a player, you may think it is easy for your student to make the transition and battle against themselves. Let's see how you do.

If you are an early bird and like to wake up early every day, I challenge you to sleep in until 11 a.m. one Saturday to see if you like it or not. I'm an early bird, so I can assure you that I know how you feel just thinking about it.

I'm not telling the early birds to wake up late every Saturday to be a better parent or partner. But if your family wants to sleep in one Saturday and have a nice family breakfast together, it may be nice for you to skip that 7 mile run you've been craving all week, stay in bed with your family, and enjoy that very special Saturday time together. Or maybe you wake up at 5:30 a.m. instead of 7:30 a.m. and go for your run. By the time you finish stretching, are showered and ready to have breakfast, your family will be starting to wake up

The same applies to adults who like to sleep in. If you prefer to stay in bed until 10:30 on weekend mornings, try waking up early to join your wife or husband in their Saturday run at the park. Trust me, they will appreciate it a lot, and you will bring balance to the relationship and your family.

The point is that we need to create balance on the court and off the court. Life won't always be easy. You can ease the "painful" moments with the right state of mind and attitude toward what's happening. It's true that a person is measured not by what happens to them but HOW they react in those situations.

PERSONAL GROWTH IS THE RIGHT PATH

> "Growth is the great separator between those who succeed and those who do not. When I see a person beginning to separate themselves from the pack, it's almost always due to personal growth." – **John C. Maxwell**

If you have read anything about personal development, you may know of John C. Maxwell, an internationally known expert on leadership and personal growth. He has sold more than 25 million books. One is called INTENTIONAL LIVING: CHOOSING A LIFE THAT MATTERS.

Remember our discussion about the power of intention?
I can assure you that once you read his books, you will start evaluating the way you think and live. He promotes creative thinking. He recommends we question everything, because most of us believe what we see and hear without really researching it

Tennis players should not depend exclusively on coaches for their training and education, and coaches should promote personal growth. Players should investigate the sport, patterns, and percentages. They should consider the reasons behind the decisions they make to understand themselves, their bodies, their game, and tennis itself. In short, each player should become experts in the sport. Coaches should serve as mentors and not act like baby sitters carrying bags and picking up balls. Players should mature along the journey of becoming a professional – and certainly after they have become pros.

> "DEFEAT IS A STATE OF MIND; NO ONE IS EVER DEFEATED UNTIL DEFEAT HAS BEEN ACCEPTED AS A REALITY."
> – **Bruce Lee**

It is clear Novak Djokovic is following this path. Many people criticize him and his performance, but I ask you:

Is Novak really losing?

He may be losing tennis matches, but as a human being, he is GROWING exponentially in comparison to other players. His priorities have changed. He wants a team, a coach, or a mentor who understands and supports the metamorphosis he is going through. This will make him feel even more balanced about his decisions and priorities. If he works with someone who sees the sport not as a way to achieve trophies and money, but as a venue to project himself into a different level of human being and as a venue to make him grow, Novak will start enjoying the game again and probably will perform better. I can almost assure you that Novak is not focusing on winning right now. I bet he is focusing on HOW he wins or HOW he lost: what emotions the match brought, when he hesitated, when he trusted himself, when he lacked confidence, and why. He is not looking at patterns and percentages and blaming the weather conditions or pain in his body, etc. He is trying to see WHAT caused the pain and why he allowed his mind to play tricks on him. I believe Novak is following the right path, because he is focused on the inside and not the outside.

> "Goals are a means to an end, not the ultimate purpose of our lives. They are simply a tool to concentrate our focus and move us in a direction. The only reason we really pursue a goal is to cause ourselves to expand and grow". – **Tony Robbins**

This brings me to an interesting point about tennis that may be true – or maybe not. I've been wondering why coaches, TV commentators, and parents tell players to hit deep on the court because PROFESSIONALS DO IT ALL THE TIME.

Do not believe everything you hear.

I encourage you to study a game of tennis and write down how many balls bounce deep on the court. Get a calculator and figure the percentages. You may be surprised.

I have done this several times, and I have NEVER been able to get a percentage higher than 31 percent. So maybe professional players do not hit deep on the court ALL THE TIME.

In fact, most tennis balls bounce in the middle of the court because professional players use a lot of spin and acceleration. It's physics. The flatter you hit, the higher the risk that the ball won't rotate, creating friction with the air. Chances are great that you will miss or hit with very big margins of error. Otherwise, why do you think players use the "kick/spin serve" as a second serve? It's physics.

Obviously, sometimes the ball bounces deeper and close to the baseline, but I can guess most players are not aiming at the line. The same thing happens with shots bouncing close to the sidelines.

Most balls bounce at least three or four feet from the line until the players start risking, based on the point situation, where they are standing on the court, the score, and the need.

If they have risked too much, they know it, and they do not like it, as you will see from their reaction. At that time, when they risked too much, they have eaten a BIG COOKIE! And you don't want to eat cookies, especially at important moments in a match. It's like eating cookies the weeks before your wedding.

I can assume players never aim to the lines, with the exception of the serve. The players hit to the chosen side with nice margins to prevent errors, but sometimes the balls bounce close to the lines. If you are a player, you know this. When you play doubles, you are not aiming to the lines, but sometimes you actually hit them, and you get a standing ovation from your supporters who are watching the game and drinking a margarita.

Committing to your personal growth may benefit your game more than anything else. It brings awareness, which causes you to make better decisions. When a person is mature, you can trust their decisions.

When juniors are learning through losses, they are putting this concept in practice. If they play a more consistent player and lose badly, they will try next time to be more consistent or to move to the net and apply pressure. If they forget what they are supposed to do next time, they are not growing; life stays the same. Human beings are the only species that make the same mistake more than once. A dog will never fall in the same hole twice.

Growing up takes time, and if you don't think so, look at the British pro, Andy Murray. He is not a junior anymore. He is maturing, therefore he is getting better results. But when he doesn't control his emotions and starts cussing at his box and insulting everyone, he does not perform at his best.

He is so talented, and he can win even if he insults the entire world, but is he becoming a better PERSON during that match?

Andy Murray is amazing to watch. I truly enjoy his game, especially when I see him smile and enjoy the match. It is as if he has an extra gear. When his emotions are controlled and positive, he starts flying at a higher level, like a racehorse when the jockey allows him to let loose.

> *"How you think about a problem is more important than the problem itself." – Norman Vincent Peale*

Maria Sharapova has returned to the tour after being penalized for consuming what some considered a prohibited performance-enhancing product.

I'm not supporting the consumption of any performance enhancers and I think only Maria knows what happened. But I want to show how other players are seeing the situation, and how it has become a problem for them.

Some of them do not agree that she should be getting wild cards to Stuttgart, Madrid, and other tournaments, and we probably can agree with them.

However, what if these players were in her shoes? Would they like a couple of wild cards? Probably yes.

They can see this "problem" as an opportunity to prove that they can play her now, and without consuming any performance enhancers, they can win against her. Or, if they cannot win, they can at least conduct an honorable battle on the court and indirectly help her get back on her feet after the mistake she made. It would be nice to see that level of maturity on the tour.

SOMETIMES WE WIN, SOMETIMES WE LEARN

When you have played tennis, you know how complicated it is to win and get consistent results. Losing can take a toll on you. If you allow all the losses to creep into your being, it can be devastating emotionally.

When kids in school have a test in any subject and they do not get an "A" on that particular test, what happens? The student receives the scored test, analyzes it, sees where he made mistakes, studies those parts more, makes notes, and learns from his mistakes to prevent them from happening again on the next test.

I ask my tournament players to make notes of every match to learn from their experiences. In the same way they take notes in school, they should take notes in tennis practices and during competition. Consider these notes from one of my players:

Sunday May 14th
I was not spinning my second serve enough, and she attacked it. I need to work on it in the coming weeks. More spin, more acceleration, better aiming, variety.

I had a lot of choices to move into the net during pressure times, but I stayed back because I didn't want to lose the point. I want to train all month on approaches and moving into the net to build confidence and be ready to execute during pressure times.

I was not consistent enough, and I was playing with wrong margins. Remember – tennis is a sport of mistakes and not winners.

If a kid fails the same test or misses the same questions repeatedly in school, it would be a big deal, right?

So, if juniors go to tennis classes every day, why don't they take notes? Why don't they take their tennis lessons as seriously as school? Could tennis teach them the same or even more valuable lessons than a school test?

Why do the lessons take so much longer to learn? Probably because coaches, parents, players are focused on winning and losing, not in **LEARNING**.

> "You have to be focused on the process. You cannot be glued to the results." – **Ivan Lendle**

Results will follow if the focus changes to learning or the process. In school, kids get results in the form of grades because they focus on the class and the information, not only on the grades or results.

For that reason, I believe we should always promote learning with our players, more than the results. Learning should be a key priority after every training and every match, competition, or tournament.

My father has always told me that when a player wins, no one says too much about the match. The coach, player, parents, or team members celebrate, and there is little tendency to analyze what happened in their game and what could have been done better. Most only analyze a match when the player has lost. That's when the criticism, advice, and tips pour in.

Sometimes You Win—Sometimes You Learn: Life's Greatest Lessons Are Gained from Our Losses.

> "A problem is not really a problem unless you allow it to be a problem. A problem in reality is an opportunity. If you can always see it this way, then every time you face a problem you will understand that you are in front of an opportunity. At least it could be an opportunity to learn; however, it could become even more if you try to solve it with the right attitude." – **John C. Maxwell,**

GRATITUDE IS KEY

> *"Be thankful of what you have; you will end up having more. If you concentrate on what you don't have, you will never, ever have enough."* – **Oprah Winfrey**

People are starting to understand that this life has some rules we need to follow in order to find balance. Practicing gratitude is one.

Every time Juan Martin Del Potro wins, he makes the sign of the cross and looks up into the sky. He says some words and then walks straight to the net to shake the opponent's hand. How nice of a gesture is that! I wonder why most of us do not do it on a daily basis: during practices, during fitness training, during lunch, during work hours, etc. Some people pray, and I think it is something very similar.

Soccer pro "El Chicharito" Hernandez prays before every match. He gets lots of criticism for that and for the way he plays. They say he is not that talented and that he is lucky and weak, but guess what? He is not even thirty years old, and he is already the greatest goal scorer in the history of the Mexican National Team.

I explained to my older students the concept of gratitude with the following example:

If you are a little kid, maybe seven years old, and you want to start playing any sport, you go to your father and say to him, "Dad, please can you buy me those tennis shoes? I want to start training and I need them!"

Your father probably will say YES and will buy you the shoes if that's really what you want to do. When your dad buys that pair of shoes, you will give him a huge hug and kiss and will tell him, "Thanks dad!"

If after three months of daily training your shoes get a hole, you may ask your dad to buy you new shoes. Guess what he will say if he sees you've been working hard and were thankful when he bought them the first time? He will say yes.

But, if after he buys the first pair, you only mumble your thanks one time, and you don't give him a kiss and hug and run away, he may wonder if you were really conscious about his effort and if you were thankful.

And what if, after he gets you the second pair of shoes, you stop training every day and start missing practices, but you ask for a new pair because your friends got the new style? Probably your father will say yes, but he will ask you why you need them if the shoes do not have holes and you are not practicing as much.

If you say because your friends have the new style shoes and you want them, maybe your father will buy another pair of shoes. But he will tell you to make sure to use them and practice consistently before he will buy other pair.

But what if you receive the new pair of shoes and don't even say thanks? You just grab the box of shoes and run away to show the shoes to your friends.

Do you think your father will buy you any more shoes? No way.

God blesses us with health, food, shelter, jobs, family, etc. Not only do we not give thanks daily, but sometimes we even complain about these things. How do we expect the Father to bless us with more?

I ask why don't we give thanks every day during tennis or fitness?

Coaches, players, and parents should incorporate a gratitude practice into their routine.

Consider this example:

A player has been training for the last five years with the same coach. Most players and parents will think that after five years, the player needs a change and some fresh input to keep improving. The player may get "tired" of the same routines and type of coaching and may complain silently or vocally by communicating his dissatisfaction to his friends and family.

I believe if this is the case, the chances of getting a better coach decrease. They may get a new coach, but a better one? I'm not sure. Have you ever heard the phrase THE TEACHER APPEARS WHEN THE STUDENT IS READY?

I believe that if you are thankful for your coach, and you have maximized him/her, and you continue to be thankful, a better coach will show up who is right for you and your personal development.

Do you think it is a coincidence that Nadal and Djokovic kept their coaches for years and years? I think Nadal and Djokovic are evolving and soon will need a new team or at least some fresh air or perspective to keep growing. The right person will not appear until they are one hundred percent grateful for what they have now.

Now consider a technical example of the power of gratitude.

A player has a phenomenal forehand. His backhand for some reason -- technical, physical, tactical, or different point of view -- is not as good, and the player and coach don't consider it a weapon. They keep working to make it better. The player complaints every time he loses that his backhand keeps him from advancing in levels. They can continue to work at it and find more problems with his backhand, or they can keep trying to find ways to make it better. I think that's a good idea and would support it. However, what if they are losing the fact that he has an awesome forehand?

Don't you think they should focus on how to maximize that side and be thankful for it?

Imagine Roger Federer worrying so much about his one-handed backhand that he forgets about how amazing his forehand is? If Roger is thankful and feels gratitude for how great his forehand is, he will be able to use it wisely and maximize his stroke and weapon to dictate his game and strategy based on it. If he does that, his forehand will continue to improve and allow him to attack or get out of trouble. His game will grow stronger. Probably most influential athletes in history have that positive mindset engraved in their DNA.

Some coaches will say to keep it simple; focus on maximizing your strengths and hiding as much as possible your weaknesses. I support that. However, the feeling of gratitude is not included in these common sports concepts.

The feeling of gratitude changes your frequency. Your particles start vibrating at a different level, and the way you feel will change. This frequency change will help you attract better and more positive situations and people to your life.

Research demonstrates that gratitude can significantly improve your health, develop better and positive emotions, improve relationships, and deal with adversity, including playing tennis.

THE COMPLAINING ERA

> "If you found yourself in paradise, it wouldn't be long before your mind would say, "Yes, but..." – **Eckhart Tolle**

I'm not sure if you have noticed, but many people now live in a complaining world. Their point of view about everything is negative. From the moment they wake up, they are focused on all the bad things they can see.

"I'm tired... it's too early to wake up... I'm so hungry... same breakfast as yesterday... my clothes are wrinkled... rush hour and traffic are making me crazy... I do not like my boss... the coach is too strict...

my classmates are not good enough... the tennis balls are bouncing too much... my strings stink... it's too windy... the economy is awful... my family doesn't support me... my girlfriend is too picky... my students are OCD... the school principal is always checking... there are no good programs on TV... the weather is so hot... the weather is too cold... the service in this restaurant is horrible... my salary is not high enough... the coach doesn't understand my kid... the parents don't respect my coaching... the student never listens to me... I'm so sore from yesterday's workout... the same drill is annoying me... we do not train enough serves... I'm so tired at the end of the day...." You get the idea.

No doubt, you have heard that everything is energy, that our thoughts travel at different frequencies and they affect our reality. This has been scientifically proven through magnetic resonance imaging that analyzes what parts of the brain get activated depending on the actions, thoughts or dreams of the subject. It has been said that the brain cannot tell the difference between dreams, thoughts, and reality. That's why some coaches promote visualization, even with Olympians and high-performance athletes.

Source: "Olympians use imagery as Mental Training" - **New York Times / https://www.nytimes.com/2014/02/23/sports/olympics/olympians-use-imagery-as-mental-training.html**

Source: Does your brain distinguish real from imaginary? *Published on* **October 30, 2014** *by* **David R. Hamilton PhD http://drdavidhamilton.com/does-your-brain-distinguish-real-from-imaginary/**

Negative thoughts and statements affect us energetically. That's why most people feel drained at the end of the day, even if they have a good eating plan and they exercise enough. Positive thoughts not only change your mentality or attitude, but they help you physically.

When people complain, they create a sense of lack. For example, if they complain about their salary, they are creating mentally a lack of funds to pay all their bills. If they complain about being too cold, they are creating shortage of warmth. If they complain about not having enough competition, they are creating the shortage for learning something every time they play an opponent, no matter how strong.

Take as an example people from a "poor" country like Nigeria, Ecuador, or Nicaragua. Some of the people living in those countries do not have the luxury of warm water to shower every day. Many do not have a car to drive to work or even a job. So, they don't have water, they don't have a car, they don't have a job, but they still wake up with a positive attitude, thinking they will have a better day than yesterday They will make the most of their day to bring food to the table for their kids.

I see now small countries such as Croatia, France, Czech Republic and others creating way more players than big countries that have all what is needed to create and develop pro players. Very interesting.

How are you going to see the world, your practice, and your matches? How about your coach, your students, or your parents?

When you complain, you are doing exactly the opposite from being thankful. Why do you expect things to improve?

It is impossible to be thankful and to complain at the same time. It is not natural.

Imagine getting new shoes from your father or sponsor and thanking them. Then, when they leave, you complain about the colors and style. Are you really thankful? It's a contradiction, and it's easy to see.

Or, imagine a family praying before a meal in a restaurant, thanking God for providing the food, but twenty minutes later some of them complain that the main course is lacking flavor and seasoning.

It's crazy!

If this is happening, it's clear to see it is a contradiction. If the seasoning is not ideal for them, they can just ask for salt and pepper or ask the chef to make some changes, but complaining should not be part of the equation.

You cannot be thankful and complain at the same time. This applies to many different topics.

If you are part of an environment that is negative, remove yourself from it. It is contagious. Leaving it is the best antidote.

> "Go 24 hours without complaining. (Not even once). Then watch how your life starts changing." – **Katrina Mayer**

I AM

> "*I am the Greatest.*" – ***Muhammad Ali***

As Buddha said; what you think you become. For that reason, it is very important to use the words **I AM** very carefully.

If someone says, "I AM a choker," then, the idea or thought becomes a fact and therefore a reality.

With a positive state of mind, we can always use the words I AM correctly, even for a challenging situation.

If your serve is not ideal and your toss is not consistent, you have two choices. You can say "I AM not serving well," or "I AM improving my serve."

Your point of view can change everything. Will you be positive or negative? A victim or a builder?

I'm sure that if we extend the topic of the concept of I AM, we can probably write an entire book about it, but I think it is very clear and simple.

Look what Rhonda Byrnes, the author of "The Secret" and famous for explaining the law of attraction says about the words I AM.

> "When you say "I AM" the words that follow are summoning creation with a mighty force, because you are declaring it to be fact." – **Rhonda Byrne**

I've seen several tennis players with lots of talent, with potential to reach high levels of tennis. They are very competitive and at an early age and specially during the normal maturity process when they are changing from boys to young men, they have a tendency to be hard on themselves and when they lose important points or when they are facing adversity, they usually make the mistake of saying things such as: I AM a terrible player! I AM a choker! I AM going to lose! I AM so bad! I AM Weak!

If they would understand how powerful those words are, they will not repeat that mistake ever again.

Notice sometimes how some people say "I AM going to get sick" You know what happens right?

Exactly!

ROUTINES OF THE SUCCESSFUL MINDS

When I talk about successful routines in tennis, I am not talking about moving bottles around, asking for the towel after every point, cleaning the clay from the lines before serving, not stepping on lines, and so forth. I think such routines can help players stay in the present moment, however, they can be dangerous in the long term if you do not learn to face your fears.

The routines I want to suggest now are those that successful people follow during morning hours, right when they wake up:

Being grateful for all you have (5-10 minutes)
Health
Oxygen
A heartbeat

Food
House
Family
School
Job
Coach, Students, etc.
Conscious breathing routine (5-10 minutes)
Writing new ideas in a journal (5-10 minutes)
Analyzing your fears in detail so you can realize they are non-existent most of the time. (5-10 minutes)
Listening to high frequency music
Watching motivational or personal growth videos (30 + minutes)
Exercising (running, yoga, weights, cycling, swimming, etc.)
Source: Book - "Tools of Titans" – Tim Ferris

Tim Ferriss, author of THE 4-HOUR WORKWEEK is an entrepreneur who works as adviser for some of the most powerful companies in the world.

He found such routines to be important to some 200 top performers he interviewed for his book TOOLS OF TITANS: THE TACTICS, ROUTINES AND HABITS OF BILLIONAIRES, ICONS, AND WORLD-CLASS PERFORMERS. Ferris says more than 84 percent of the most successful people in the world do some type of mindfulness routine every day.

Source: https://www.thriveglobal.com/stories/18602-what-tim-ferriss-and-some-of-the-world-s-most-successful-people-do-every-morning

I personally think that the concept of staying in the present should not be called Mindfulness for lots of reasons. Maybe one day I will explain all the reasons in a different book.

While you develop your mindfulness skills and habits, I also recommend daily sessions in which you consciously focus your mind on the good things you want to achieve or the things you are grateful for. Make those thoughts always positive. If you continue to do this in a disciplined way, you will attract more of what you are thinking about, because that's how the Universe works. Some call it the Law of Attraction. We can call it faith, focus or concentration, but it must be incorporated in our sport as a daily training routine.

> "See yourself living in abundance and you will attract it. It works every time, with every person." – **Bob Proctor**

To achieve higher levels in anything, you must get to know your mind and train your mind. With time, you will become what you have been thinking, consciously and unconsciously.

Obviously, it is better to do it consciously to manifest positive things.

This rule can apply to tennis easily in terms of developing a great preparation, rotation, and follow through. It can help you be a great tactician and improve your fitness. Start by seeing the best that you can be. Start by imagining that best version of yourself, and then train mentally and physically every day to achieve it.

7

Levels Of Emotions

Water, Fear, Courage, Pride, Joy & Injuries

> *"Dear GOD, please grant me the strength and Serenity to accept things I cannot change, The COURAGE to change the things I can and The WISDOM to know the difference." –* **Unknown**

I believe this chapter is important and if you understand it, it will change your life forever. If you get nothing else from this book, LEARN this chapter and you will be more balanced one day.

I think we all can agree that emotions are very important for all of us. Whether we have positive or negative emotions, all of them can have a positive or negative impact on us. It all depends on the point of view of the person that is feeling a specific emotion.

As with words, emotions can cause major physical and chemical changes in our body.

Before I share with you an experiment done by a Japanese doctor, you probably already know that close to 70% of our body is water.

"According to H.H. Mitchell, Journal of Biological Chemistry 158, the brain and heart are composed of 73% water, and the lungs are about 83%

water. The skin contains 64% water, muscles and kidneys are 79%, and even the bones are watery: 31%."

Source: **https://water.usgs.gov/edu/propertyyou.html**

Water is so important that we all know that if we find water in any other planet, the chances of finding any type of life in that planet increases exponentially.

Water is essential to our life and most people relate water only with hydration or dehydration levels. Even some of the best doctors in the world probably do not know the important the information below. I really want to share this with the most people possible because it is so important.

Dr. Emoto did hundreds of experiments by freezing little containers of water and looking with a high tech microscope at the frozen crystals that were created.

He used several different types of water such as tap water, water from rivers close to big cities, water from lakes away from society, etc. He also wrote words such as: love, hate, caring, patience, ugly and so on in the containers to see if the words created different results in the frozen crystals.

Dr. Emoto was not able to see pretty crystals from tap water and water from rivers or lakes close to big cities. On the other hand, he saw magnificent crystals from clean pure water from rivers and lakes away from big cities.

After the initial experiments Dr. Emoto decided to offer pure prayers to the "dirty or contaminated" water, to speak good words and play nice music to it. The results were astonishing. The crystals changed and became beautiful.

He also decided to tape negative words to some clean water containers such as: hate, shame and so forth, play heavy metal and guess what happened?

The crystals changed and lost form and looked ugly under the microscope and also it is important to know that from all experiments, they never saw identical crystals.

All this happened in 1994 and after that, there have been more people doing the experiments and confirming all this is true. Some people have tried to debunk the concept but I choose to believe it is true because water is also energy and energy transforms based on what is around it.

However, even if Dr. Emoto's experiment is not accurate, we know our bodies are at least 70% water and we know there is positive and negative energy. We are energy and energy transforms. It is common sense that if our energy is negative, we will cause a change in our body because our bodies and cells vibrate and feed from energy. It's all connected.

Another good video that I highly recommend is the one from Laureate Luc Montagnier (Nobel Prize)

Source: Water Memory - (Documentary of 2014 about Nobel Prize laureate Luc Montagnier)

Source: https://www.youtube.com/watch?v=R8VyUsVOic0

If you are taking all this seriously, you may have watched the video from Dr. Emoto so now translate this to tennis.

Can you imagine all the negative impact we can create with our players and kids when we tell them things such as: You don't know how to compete, your strokes looked awful today, what a shame, it was a terrible match, you're out of shape, you were choking, etc.

And what about when we criticize ourselves inside or outside the court with comments such as: what an idiot, you stink, you are stupid, what a dumb decision, I choked, I was afraid, my serve stinks, etc.

People use the word "hate" like it is nothing. They use it on the court to criticize drills or strokes or at a restaurant to criticize food or service or while watching TV to criticize shows, movies, commercials, etc. I think you get my point. They use the word so lightly and they have no idea they are affecting themselves internally because their particles start vibrating differently and their "crystals" will not be balanced.

This relates to injuries also. Take as an example, Andy Murray and his temperament and what happened to him this year (2017) when he contracted shingles. In the Telegraph from the United Kingdom they were mentioning that maybe Andy was pushing himself too hard in training.

This is a way of blaming the work he puts on and off the court but if the concept about water is true, all his emotions, the cussing and yelling could be the actual source of the problem.

Source: http://www.telegraph.co.uk/tennis/2017/02/26/andy-murray-shakes-shingles-step-back-treadmill-dubai-tournament/

For those of you who don't know, shingles is common in people over 55-65 years old. It supposed to be the virus we kept dormant after we contract chickenpox but it comes back or activates itself when your immune system is weak because of stress.

If this is true, why is Andy activating the virus? Think about it for a minute. Could it be the stress and negative emotions he feels on the court?

When I was younger, I didn't even know the word stress. However, today it is so common that even doctors tell their patients that stress is the cause of the majority of health problems.

I heard a 20 year old say recently that her doctor told her she has scoliosis because of stress. So I ask everyone, what is unnecessary stress if not a NEGATIVE EMOTION?

Another good example is Tomy Haas. The first time I saw him in person was in Houston in the Clay Court Pro Tournament. Tomy was already in his thirties and I heard that he had struggled with many injuries or surgeries during his tennis career. When I saw him, he was training during the weekend before the Main Draw was going to start. He had no t-shirt on and I could see that he was a very talented athlete. You could not ask for a better tennis physique and frame. He had muscles everywhere, was elastic on the court, explosive, fluid, and strong. When I saw he was so strong I started questioning why he gets injured and some players with weaker bodies were healthier than him.

It made no sense.

That's when I started reading about kinesiology and especially applied kinesiology.

Dr. David R Hawkins (M.D., Ph.D) has an amazing book I mentioned before called "Power vs. Force."

In that book, there is a chapter called "Power and Sports" and he says very important things I will mention below, but first you have to understand and read a graph he calls: "Map of Consciousness"

Map of Consciousness

GOD-View	Life-View	Level	Scale	Emotion	Process
Self	Is	Enlighten	700 <	Ineffable	Pure-Consciousness
All-Being	Perfect	Peace	600	Bliss	Illumination
One	Complete	Joy	540	Serenity	Transfiguration
Loving	Benign	Love	500	Reverence	Revelation
Wise	Meaningful	Reason	400	Understanding	Abstraction
Merciful	Harmonious	Acceptance	350	Forgiveness	Transcendence
Inspiring	Hopeful	Willingness	310	Optimism	Intention
Enabling	Satisfactory	Neutrality	250	Trust	Release
Permitting	*Feasible*	*Courage*	*200*	*Affirmation*	*Empowerment*
Indifferent	Demanding	Pride	175	Scorn	Inflation
Vengeful	Antagonistic	Anger	150	Hate	Aggression
Denying	Disappointing	Desire	125	Craving	Enslavement
Punitive	Frightening	Fear	100	Anxiety	Withdrawal
Disdainful	Tragic	Grief	75	Regret	Despondency
Condemning	Hopeless	Apathy	50	Despair	Abdication
Vindictive	Evil	Guilt	30	Blame	Destruction
Despising	Miserable	Shame	20	Humiliation	Elimination

See how high the level of **PEACE** is located in the Map? It's in the 600's. Now, read what Roger Federer has to say about peace:

> "Once you find that peace, that place of peace and quiet, harmony and confidence, that's when you start playing your best." – **Roger Federer.**

There is good information about this map in the following links:

Sources: http://www.artofwellbeing.com/2016/11/08/mapofconsciousness/

https://personalexcellence.co/blog/map-of-consciousness/

If you notice in the map; the level of emotions that move you from negative to positive is **COURAGE.** And the emotion or level that allows you to rise to courage is PRIDE.

It's clear to see how **COURAGE** can change a match and that's why everyone in the sport promotes "fighting" in a match and trying to overcome the obstacles you face. If you have no courage, how can you win a match?

> "Encourage Courage." – **Dr. Robert Sones**

That's why a lot of new age psychologists, spiritual or personal growth coaches work with their clients on repeating affirmations. At the courage level, affirmations as you can see in the graph are the emotions attached to the Level of Courage.

- I can do this!
- C'mon!
- Let's Go!
- VAMOS!
- Ale!

But did you see what level and emotions go below Pride? It's Anger and Hate. Remember the water experiment and what the word or feeling of anger or hate does to the water crystals? Now imagine how Andy Murray's negative emotions affect him physically. Tomy Hass also has a strong personality and if all this is true and accurate, it makes a lot of sense why Tomy has been through so many injuries.

Do you understand? That's why some players get more injuries than others. No one explores these internal reasons. They focus only on external reasons such as muscles, technique, overloads, ligaments, etc.

And that's not only the sad part, but also the way they treat the injury because they don't treat injuries based on the source. Most doctors prescribe anti-inflammatories, ask the patient to rest and then start physical rehab.

I have played tennis since I was 7, and by the time I was 25 most doctors told me my back was a mess and that I should not run, lift or play tennis anymore because my spine had bulged discs and fractures.

I treated the pain like most people do by visiting doctors, getting cortisone shots, doing rehab, stretching, exercises, and so on and my pain never went away. I had back pain for 10 years and it got so bad that I was not able to stand on one foot and put my pants on. I had to sit, otherwise it was impossible. After 10 years of spending lots of money, you know what cured me?

I read a book by Dr. John E. Sarno called "Healing Back Pain" that explained in detail how our physical pain comes from emotional pain.

After I read the book I was cured. I couldn't even believe it at the beginning and kept hesitating and wondering why my pain went away. Since then, I've been coaching tennis for 10 years, I've done triathlons and I'm physically active almost every day.

The book doesn't just focus on the spine or back but any type of pain that appears like knee, wrist, ankle, neck pain, etc. Sometimes my back hurts a bit but I don't pay attention to it. Instead, I analyze what I have been feeling or thinking and it goes away.

Maybe you won't believe me at first but I challenge you to read the book if you have had chronic pain, and you will be impressed. Some friends and family members have been cured also because they read it and had an open mind.

> *"Our diagnosis and treatment of Tension Myositis Syndrome represent another yet another instance of what is possible when the power of the mind is mobilized for healing the body. It's not magic; it is as scientific as the appropriate use of antibiotics, for science encompasses everything that is true in nature."* – **John E. Sarno**

Going back to the Map, If you analyze it even further, you will see the level or emotion of **FEAR** is vibrating at a lower level than courage. We all know that in tennis, the moment you start feeling fear about anything, you will not perform well. Some call it *"choking."*

Now, that you have seen the map of consciousness, maybe you understand why Djokovic hired a "Love Guru".

Most people think Novak "Nole" Djokovic is not making wise decisions now, but although he may not be performing as well as before, he is becoming a better person. He understands that life has physical laws and that more you get aligned with them, the better you will feel and do.

It is interesting he hired a Love Guru since Love is one of the highest Levels in the Map of Consciousness. That tells me that Novak is trying to gain knowledge and to grow as a person.

The fact that he hired Andre Agassi also tells you he is on the right track. Andre said in his book that he didn't like tennis. It seems he had a lot of pressure from his father and that affected him a lot. Andre is an amazing human being and now his purpose is greater than tennis. Andre and his wife, who is one of the best players in history, are focused on giving kids the chance to have a good education and start in life.

If my predictions are right, Novak hired him because Andre will not focus on technique or any other external factor but rather, he will focus on growth, maturity, joy, peace, and so on.

In her book, "The Power," Rhonda Byrne writes:

LOVE RULES

> "There is one rule with money: you can never put money ahead of love. If you do, you violate love's law of attraction, and you will suffer the consequences. **Love must be the ruling force in your life.** Nothing can ever be put above love. Money is a tool for you to use, and you bring it to yourself through love, but if you put money ahead of love in your life, it will cause you to receive a whole bunch of negative things. You can't give love for money and then walk around being rude and negative to people, because if you do that, you open the door for negativity to walk into your relationships, health, happiness, and finances." – **Rhonda Byrne.**

Remember the Map of consciousness and where Love stands? Everything is related and the more we know it and the more aware we are, the more we will help not only the sport of tennis but other sports and the entire world. Tennis can be the first sport to help develop this world into even a better place.

If this concept is correct, then it is easy to explain why some countries that are gigantic and have all the resources needed to produce great tennis players are not able to in comparison with other small countries with less resources as I mentioned already.

Maybe in the smaller countries, their focus is NOT MONEY but rather the LOVE of the sport and how much they WANT TO HELP their players. Passion is a MUST to be a great teacher. And great teachers focus more on building the human being and not building a player or making a business out of the players.

If this is all true, that is why many successful people recommend doing the job you LOVE, because then YOU LOVE what you do and your "work" becomes your passion. And when you work on your passion, all other things will align in your life, and you will find balance and happiness.

Pride and Sports

If Dr. Sarno, and Dr. Sones are correct about emotions and how they affect our health and performance, then Dr. Hawkins explains and confirms in further detail about negative emotions and how they will make you weaker in sports:

"Through Kinesiology, we can demonstrate that <u>if one is motivated by any of the energy fields below COURAGE</u>, one goes weak. The notorious Achilles' heel <u>that brings down</u> not just athletes but the potentially great in all areas of human achievement <u>is PRIDE</u>. Pride calibrated at 175, not only makes the performer go weak, but it can't provide the motivational power of love, honor, or dedication to a higher principle (or even to excellence itself). If we ask a powerful athlete to hold in mind the hope of defeating his opponent, or becoming a star, or making a lot of money, we'll see that he goes weak and we can put down his trained, muscular arm with minimal effort. The same athlete holding in mind the honor of his country or his sport, the dedication of his performance to someone he loves, or even the sheer joy of maximum effort for the sake of excellence, goes powerfully strong, and we cannot push down his arm with even the greatest effort." -

Source: *Book "Power vs Force / The Hidden Determinants of Human Behavior" – David R. Hawkins M.D., Ph.D.*

Now, look at the Map of Consciousness and see where you find the Level of JOY. Joy is related with the emotion of SERENITY. Have you ever heard tennis players or any professional athletes respond when a reporter asks them when are they going to stop playing or competing?

They generally respond with something like: "I will stop when I'm not enjoying it anymore or when my body says stop."

Do you think it is a coincidence that they mention the emotion of joy? Everything is related and the graph from Dr. Hawkins proves it makes a lot of sense.

If you do not believe in applied kinesiology, I recommend going to a doctor that practices it. You will be surprised during the strength test: your arm will go weak depending on what you are thinking or feeling, or even touching or hearing.

See for yourself what happens when you are listening to heavy metal music. Make a friend try to push your arm down while you try to keep it without moving it at shoulder level. See what happens.

Now, do the same experiment while listening to nice piano or classical music and you will see the difference.

Also in applied kinesiology, you learn that not only are you affected by what you feel or think, but also by what people around you are feeling and thinking. It is very interesting because things that are "out of our control" can affect us also. Things that happen around us are impacting our vibration and frequency.

The amazing thing is that there is A LOT happening around us and we don't even know it. This is science and people know it but this information has not been shared in the way is supposed to. That's why it is important to find a good environment for yourself because everything around you can affect you positively or negatively, unless your state of mind is super strong, positive and your level of awareness is higher than the general population. Some other people would call it faith also, which I believe is completely accurate.

> "The environment in which we live and work is a mirror of our attitude and expectations." – **Earl Nightingale**

Read the link below and you will be impressed about how much information the brain is processing while the human eyes do not see that information. "The brain processes 400 billion bits of information a second. BUT, we are ONLY aware of 2,000 of those?" -Dr. Joseph Dispenza, D.C.

Source: **http://www.basicknowledge101.com/subjects/brain.html**

This information is amazing because we can see with our eyes a very small amount of things that are happening around us. That is why it is important to try to start training our minds to be aware and be able to control at least what we can control so that we can make an impact not only in the way we feel, think, perform and so on but also making an impact in our environment.

I will tell you a true story that happened to a student and myself on a trip when we went to play ITF in the Caribbean.

I was on the plane with two players and I believe we were on our way to Jamaica. The plane was still on the runway and two aisles behind us there was a couple with a baby that started crying as soon as we entered the plane. The plane was on the runway for a long time and then it took off and we started flying. After several minutes of listening to the baby cry, I decided to ask one of my players if she wanted to make an experiment with me. I was reading Dr. Hawkins book so I thought it would be a good idea to see if we could change the environment with the right emotions.

She agreed, so I asked her if she had noticed the baby crying. She said yes and that is has been non-stop. I said the experiment will be to send the feeling of LOVE to that baby for two minutes straight and if we truly concentrate I believed we would be able to stop the baby from crying. She agreed so I asked her to close her eyes and start sending love to the baby. I started keeping track of my watch and we started. I kept concentrating on sending love, and once in a while I opened my eyes to see if she was focused. The baby kept crying loudly and there was no positive change in the tone initially. It was actually worse. After a while, I thought we were close to the two minute mark and I open my eyes and checked my watch There were about 15 seconds left and I thought this is not working. Then I caught myself doubting, I looked at my student and she still had her eyes closed. I closed my eyes again and I told GOD that I knew he could make the baby stop crying and send love to him. When I thought 10 seconds passed by, I open my eyes again and the kid was still crying. I checked my watch and there were four seconds left. When I was about to quit and tell my student to open her eyes, the kid stopped crying completely. No sound at all and it happened right when I was touching my student's arm to make her open her eyes. When the kid stopped, she opened her eyes, I checked my watched and there were 2 seconds after the time we agreed on. My student looked at me in complete disbelief and I showed her the time. Her eyes and mouth were wide open. I asked her right at that moment: Do you believe now that what we think and feel can affect us and other people or the environment? She said "Yes!"

If you think about it, you can relate this to Faith also. What you believe IS.

8

Training and Competing with Purpose

> "There is no hope of success for the person who does not have a central purpose or definite goal at which to aim." – Napoleon Hill

Tennis is a sport of mistakes.

Think about it. Generally speaking, whoever has fewer errors wins. Coaches count the mistakes. You can even see tournaments on television that use software to count the number of unforced errors each player makes. This is not the rule, but it is a big part of the sport.

To minimize errors and increase a player's success, as a coach, the first rule I stress is to be consistent.

Next, I ask my players to be aggressive and attack in tennis. Statistics track the number of winners a player hits during a match and its ratio in comparison to unforced errors, the number of times the player goes to the net, and how many times they won out of those times.

I teach my players not to rush during matches, because when you rush, your decision-making ability is diminished, which can bring more problems or unforced errors to the match.

Let's analyze consistency, attacking, and rushing from a coach's perspective. Let's say a player is very consistent, and his mistakes are low. But he loses the match because he was not aggressive enough.

The player starts training going to the net and trying to finish easy shots to increase his winner shots. He goes to the next tournament and makes a bunch of mistakes because he was trying to hit winners. The coach tells him he lost because he was going for big shots, he made mistakes, and he was rushing.

The player gets confused and starts working on patience again, which was his natural ability in the first place. The coach continues to tell him he has to attack. But when he attacks, he is told to not rush.

Do you see what happens?

Do you think professional players are worried about how many winners they hit per match? I don't even know why someone invented that nonsense name (winners) for that type of shot and why they actually count them.

Some coaches can easily fix this by telling the player to attack with margins, but most players get confused, and sometimes they lose months or years trying to figure things out.

The same thing happens when we tell our players they should not depend on us but make their own good decisions on the court. Nevertheless, every day we tell them what to do and how to do it.

You probably know parents who want their kids to be independent, but they tell the kids exactly what to do and how, and they criticize them when they make mistakes.

We should allow players to grow, learn from their mistakes, and grow inside the court to be independent players. In tennis, coaching is not allowed, so why do we keep putting so much information in the kid's head?

It's a vicious cycle.

We create another vicious cycle with these two concepts:

- Stay in the present moment
- Think and make good decisions

How in the world can you ask a player to think and make good decision and stay in the present moment at the same time?

Does it make sense? Of course not.
You cannot do both things at the same time.

A study by Harvard psychologists found that the mind wanders 47 percent of the time. That means that half the time we are on the court practicing or competing, our mind wanders. Half of the time!

When some meditation teachers tell you to meditate, they also tell you to focus on your breathing. Therefore, you are thinking about your breathing.

It is probably impossible or very complicated not to think and that is why we have dreams. Even when we are sleeping, our mind is working. Think about that. So how in the world can we meditate and not think?

I am not saying it is not doable but when you enter that state where the Mind is quiet, it should NOT be called "Mindful"

The word *meditation* means:

- To engage in contemplation or reflection
- To engage in mental exercises
- To focus on one's thoughts

All these definitions are related to thinking.

To stay connected, in the present, concentrated, and so on is by focusing on one specific thing. It can be breathing, a mantra, a sound, the tennis ball, the direction you want to hit, your target, etc.

I call these examples of focusing *purpose* or *intention.*

It's the same as in business. The business has to have a clear intention, a goal, to have a better chance of success.

If the intention or target is not clear in the mind, how can you reach a goal?

I'm going to show you the Quote again. REMEMBER.

> "There is no hope of success for the person who does not have a central purpose or definite goal at which to aim." – **Napoleon Hill**

All successful people know this concept. If you do not believe me, ask Oprah Winfrey or watch the video below:

The Power of Intention|SuperSoulSunday|Oprah Winfrey Network: Source: https://www.youtube.com/watch?v=4iaqs4_xePk

Have you ever thought about why a high-performance player or a professional tennis player makes a mistake on the court? They already have a solid technique, they have good timing, biomechanics, feeling, point of contact, footwork, court positioning, spin, good hands or body-space knowledge, etc.

Why do they miss?

Most people would blame it on external factors, such as technique, footwork and so on. Other people who understand the mind and how it affects the other parts of the game would say the player missed because they lost focus.

I believe that's partially correct.

Let's start by finding different definitions for the words focus and purpose:

Focus:

- A subject that is being discussed or studied. The subject on which people's attention is focused.
- A main purpose or interest
- A point at which rays of light, heat, or sound meet or from which they move apart or appear to move apart; especially: the point at which an image is formed by a mirror, a lens, etc.
  Source: **https://www.merriam-webster.com/dictionary/focus**

Purpose:

1 **a)** something set up as an object or end to be **attained : INTENTION**
   b) RESOLUTION, DETERMINATION

2: a subject under discussion or an action in course of execution

Source: **https://www.merriam-webster.com/dictionary/purpose**

Do you see why I said it was partially correct?

If you noticed that the definitions of the word ***purpose*** have more related words or descriptions about what we are trying to accomplish in tennis during a point, good for you!

Players do not miss because they lose focus. They miss because they lost Focus on their purpose, which in this case can be:

- They lost aim or intention
- They lost determination about what they want to achieve
- They lost the aim or goal of what they are trying to do

When a professional makes an unforced error, it is not because they position themselves incorrectly on the court with their feet, or because their hips rotated too quickly, or because they hit late, or because they tossed the ball incorrectly. That's a Victim point of view.

If that was the case, why do club players, or junior players toss the ball awfully sometimes, but still manage to hit the serve inside the service box?

This also happens with pro players. You see Sharapova, Ivanovic, Halep and others toss the ball "imperfectly", and they still hit most serves inside the box. But when they miss one or two or three, everyone blames the mistake on the toss instead of the player's focus or purpose.

Maybe the moment they missed was because their mind went to a different place. Instead of "focusing" on the purpose, which in this case would be the box and a specific side (backhand/forehand), they are thinking about how "bad" they toss the ball or how they don't want to double fault. Their purpose – to accomplish something with their serve – disappears. Their purpose or focus goes to those specific negative thoughts.

Maybe the thoughts are not even negative. Maybe they are just thinking it's 3-4 in games, it's the third set, and they are a bit tired. Or maybe they are thinking about how hot it is.

If you have competed in tennis or any other sport, you know it is not simple to focus your mind for long periods. Even in school when your teacher is talking, most of the information is not sinking in because you concentrate for two minutes and then you are thinking you are hungry, or about the guy that is sitting next to you that is loud, or the way they are dressed or how they move, etc.

In tennis, why do those mistakes appear at such high levels or even at junior levels where the player's technique is essentially developed?

These mistakes are the effect of the real cause: lack of purpose or intention.

And why does the purpose or intention go away?

The purpose or intention can go away during competition for different reasons:

- Being physically tired
- No specific purpose/strategy to follow
- No habit of training with a clear purpose
- Not knowing what the purpose should be in a particular match

However, if technique, strategy, and fitness are present, the most common reason purpose disappears in competition is conscious or unconscious fear.

If you are a player, I can assure you that you have experienced this scenario:

You are playing a good point. Suddenly, you hit a ball that doesn't have enough juice to keep your opponent back, and he decides to move in to the net. The opponent doesn't hit a fantastic shot. He just hits a ball to your backhand and moves in. For some reason, even though you were comfortable, balanced and ready to hit, you rushed and hit your backhand into the net or over-hit and sent it close to the back fence. If you had that backhand and the opponent was staying back, the chances of missing would be much lower, but the "pressure" rushed you. We can even "blame" the mistake to our egos because when someone is putting pressure on us, we feel like fighting back out of pride and this will end up in a mistake.

High-level players with more experience will react differently to that approach shot. They will stay cool, choose a side/purpose to hit, and force the opponent to hit an extra shot – a volley or overhead.

These mistakes happen even at the professional level. So how do you train yourself from going nuts, making a bad decision, and rushing?

Most coaches will just say "Don't rush!" But that is easier said than done.

You must manage your fear. Tennis is similar to boxing in this aspect. In boxing, you cannot step into the ring with a fear of getting punched.

Imagine a boxer afraid of getting punched! He will get knocked out so quickly he will not know what happened.

That's what happens when a player faces someone with more experience or with a higher ranking, even if their strokes, fitness, and game are similar. The lower-ranked player freaks out during the first games because the more experienced player is more aware of a particular situation and has been in that moment more times.

This happens all the time at every level. Two players at similar levels face each other for what should be a competitive and even match. But the match is over in half an hour, and the loser doesn't know what happened.

Fear happened. Fear comes from the ego and desire for control.

In tennis, we can't control the opponent's actions or decisions. We can try to influence their decisions, but that's about it.

It's the same in boxing. A boxer cannot control what the opponent is going to throw at him. He can only control his punches and how he reacts when the opponent throws punches at him. He must accept that he will get punched, because that's what boxing is all about.

Tennis is also about getting punched. An opponent will attack, hit a better shot, serve better, return better, be more patient, etc. Understanding this enables players to be responsible for their actions. Successful players – and coaches – must not blame mistakes and bad decisions on rackets, wind, noise, positioning, balance, and other excuses.

It is imperative to train with a clear purpose and take tennis classes as seriously as a class in school or a class for a real estate license or a tennis or fitness coaching licensing class.

Boxers sometimes win fights against an opponent who is naturally stronger or has a better jab or uppercut. How? Because they stay calm and positive, they do not fear, and they stay focused by executing their strategy all the time.

Tennis is no different. How does Rafael Nadal win against players with better serves? Having a better serve is like having a better jab. Roger Federer doesn't have the best serve or backhand. However, he uses those strokes more strategically than most.

Have you noticed how easy is for Federer to win against a serve and volley player like Alexander Zverev?

When Zverev attacks and goes to the net, Federer does not panic. He takes his time, looks at the ball, chooses a side or purpose, and hits that ball easily, like he is training.

But when Federer faces Rafael "Rafa" Nadal, and Nadal is coming to the net, sometimes he panics. I personally think he does so because of the respect he has for Nadal. That respect also can be called fear: fear of Nadal finishing the point at the net, or fear of making a mistake, and so on.

Another good example of purpose is how Federer won against Nadal in the 2017 Australian Open.

Federer won because he had a specific purpose or tactics he followed almost perfectly. Perhaps his coach studied the situation and decided Federer could win against Nadal by changing his patterns with his backhand. Federer had to hit down the line with his one-handed spin backhand. Then stay closer to the line to prevent Nadal's spin developing too much and hit the slice that he used to hit that rarely affects Nadal.

Once Federer executed the down the line backhand, a box of opportunities opened because Nadal was forced to hit cross court to Federer's sweet forehand. If Nadal didn't hit a good cross court backhand, Federer could attack with his forehand to Nadal's forehand because the court was open and move forward or he could hit behind Nadal to get him off balance. It was a beauty to see how "focused" Federer was executing that strategy or purpose.

It was great to see how Federer had the purpose to attack the net hitting to the same side repeatedly until the end of the first set. Once Nadal realized what was happening, Federer changed it up, and with variety made it impossible for Nadal to get into the match and compete like usually does.

This may have been Federer's best tennis match in terms of executing purpose/tactics. Perhaps in that match, Federer finally believed there was a way to win against Nadal, even though his backhand was "weaker" than Nadal's.

Deciding what to do with a match and our opponent is like life. We can blame circumstances and situations, or we can us them to improve us and learn from them.

Life is always happening for us, not to us. It's our job to find out where the benefit is. If we do, life is magnificent. – **Tony Robbins**

Tony Robbins may be the world's most famous performance coach. He has three tips that can help you understand how to bring purpose to your tennis game.

- "Stressed" is the achiever's word for fear.
- Losers react, leaders anticipate.
- Mastery doesn't come from an infographic. What you know doesn't mean anything.

What do you do consistently?

When you develop the habit of playing with purpose, you increase your concentration and focus. We can train with a variety of purposes:

- Technical Purpose
- Physical Purpose

- Tactical Purpose
- Mental Purpose

Most players or coaches focus on technical training. It can improve if they have a system to train and develop mental habits for muscle or technical results.

For example, if a player hits a ball late and not in front as most coaches would prefer, the coach generally would say some of the following:

- You hit late!
- Prepare on time!
- Rotate your shoulders in advance
- Turn before the ball bounces on your side

When this happens, the player starts thinking and starts to "prepare" on time, but there is no mental structure to build the habit. So in 5-10 minutes they will get corrected again.

The player should understand the purpose. To execute it, the player must think about it every time he is about to hit. It is easy to lose focus because the mind is so active. This, plus the fact that coaches keep correcting different technical aspects, makes the process more complicated for the players.

If the player concentrates on that specific purpose, and they keep preparing on time or rotating their shoulders before the ball bounces, but they hit a shot and the ball goes out, the coach may say, "Spin the ball more or get under the ball more" and guess what happens? The player will focus on spinning more and will forget about rotating. The entire process can be frustrating.

I believe coaches and players should mix and train most if not all four purposes at a time. This is possible if the mind remains focused on one thing at a time. If we want the player to focus on technique, fitness, tactics and mind, here is how the practice of rotating and preparing on time should be managed.

It is important that the player repeat with his words what he has to do until the mind acquires the information and is able to repeat it. The muscles will automatically react to the mind's orders and start developing muscle memory or habits.

We do this a lot with beginner players. For example, instead of focusing on the purpose of technique only, we incorporate all the ways we can create a more balanced and complete player.

When a coach focuses on a technical aspect, they can work on it for weeks, but they may not get a "positive result" with the ball, and how the ball responds to technique. The same happens when the coach focuses only on a physical aspect such as loading with the legs, recovering, a split step, etc.

An ideal scenario that focuses on all aspects would go like this:

- Player commits to repeating with words and actions what the coach is asking and wants to work on.

Long explanation example:

- Rotate/prepare on time when the ball is flying toward me. (Technical)
- Spin the ball (Technical) and put the ball inside the add court. (Tactical)
- Follow through completely. (Technical)
- Recover with two shuffles closer to the center of the court. (Physical)

Simple explanation example:

- Player repeats commands aloud during actions:
- Rotate
- Spin the ball inside
- Follow through
- Shuffle, shuffle

This process should be executed over and over again until the player can do it without saying anything aloud. The coach can start this process by working on a specific purpose and adding more every time the player accomplishes one. All this can be executed if the process is explained correctly and the player separates each part during execution until they all become almost one.

> "What you Practice Grows Stronger." – Shauna Shapiro

For example, if the player thinks and concentrates on rotating and the follow-through and forgets about spin and putting the ball inside, you know what happens? Most of the time the ball will go out or a mistake will show up. Therefore, the player must have clearly in mind each task, in order, to prevent technical, tactical, or physical mistakes. By training all the tasks in order, the player is training his mind and keeping purpose and focus for an extended time. The habit of staying "in the zone" also develops.

The Power of a Noble Purpose

Roger Federer's foundation, dedicated to educating African children, demonstrates how a noble purpose brings balance. Federer thinks beyond the sport and money. He is a balanced human being, and that's why he keeps generating success in his life.

YVES ROSSY

Yves Rossy is a pilot, known as the Jetman, who invented a series of experimental individual jet packs using carbon-fiber wings for flight. He uses his body to direct the jet pack. "In any sport where you move (surfing, windsurfing, etc.), you go where you look," Rossy said. "Where the head goes, the body goes. It's as simple as that."

It is the same in tennis and in life. You go where your head is; you go where you focus your mind and thoughts.

If you hold an idea in your head since childhood that you will get a tennis scholarship, and you keep that idea in your mind and work for it, the chances are you will achieve that. It happened to me.

When I was a kid I heard that my father had the chance to get a scholarship in an American college to play tennis but something happened to the coach right before my dad was going to sign and he was not able to get the formal offer. My father started playing tennis a bit late. He started when he was about 14 or 15 but he became obsessed about the sport and trained every time he had a chance. He end up playing a couple of Grand Prix Tournaments locally and traveled around South American playing for Ecuador. He also became National Champion of 30 years & Older in Ecuador. He was very talented physically and mentally.

When I heard that story when I was about 9 or 10 years old, I remember thinking to myself and saying "I will get a scholarship in the USA". It's interesting but that's all I wanted. I never dreamed about being a Pro or anything and you know what I got? I got my wish fulfilled. I came to the USA with a full tennis scholarship and now after 20 years and after analyzing lots of factors, I realized I got what I was focusing on. It was my obsession and I got it. I wonder if I would have wish for something bigger and better if I would have achieved it.

Now I understand why people say "Be Careful What You Wish For" because if you wish for something, you focus on it and work on it, the chances of getting that wish are pretty big. Some people understand this concept very clearly and they know it's a natural law but they used it for bad intentions. That's why I asked at the beginning of the book to use this information wisely.

In fact, there are plenty of books that tell you this law is true and powerful and it works. Make experiments yourself and check if it works. Do not believe me and do them yourself and you will have your answer. Focus on something for long periods of time day by day and see what happens. The internal thought and wish will make you start moving, acting upon it and creating possibilities to achieve what you want. It's amazing but to me it is pure faith.

> *"Ask and it will be given to you; seek and you will find; knock and the door will be opened to you."* – Matthew 7:7 NIV

In business or any other environment, I think it is the same. Most millionaires, best-selling authors and so on, give tips all the time about having a goal, intention, idea, or an objective in mind, focus on it constantly and invest the hard work needed to accomplish that idea.

Obviously, you cannot just dream about goals and stay at home watching TV all day. The picture, goal, or idea has to be clear in your head, and you need to take steps towards it. Even in the Bible, we can read of the importance of taking action:

> *"If one of you says to them, "Go in peace; keep warm and well fed," but does nothing about their physical needs, what good is it? In the same way, faith by itself, if it is not accompanied by action, is dead."* – James 2:16-17 NIV

Your focus, mentality, state of mind, belief, and faith determine your results. Your focus is key. Your mentality is key. What you think is key. We must train the brain and what we are thinking on a daily basis.

The Power of the Subconscious Mind

> *"You cannot entirely control your subconscious mind, but you can voluntarily hand over to it any plan, desire, or purpose which you wish transformed into concrete form."* – **Napoleon Hill**

In Chapter 4, I discussed how Napoleon Hill and Rhonda Byrne taught that belief creates reality. The concept works by training your subconscious mind. You hold in your mind a clear picture of what you want to accomplish, concentrate on your feelings when you achieve the goal, and repeat.

This system can be executed successfully in tennis to achieve technical goals, fitness goals, etc.

Let me share an example using a tennis racket. Kids implement the system naturally, without even knowing it. People stop using the system when they hear that things are NOT possible to achieve and doubt creeps inside their head.

A kid sees Rafa Nadal's new tennis racket on TV. She really likes the colors and design, and she gets excited about the idea of training and competing with the racket. The kid visualizes showing her brand new, shiny racket to her friends at training. She imagines how it will feel when she unwraps the plastic that covers the grip for protection. She imagines playing with the racket; she feels herself on the court with it. She talks about it to her friends, brothers, sisters, and parents before and after practice.

She tells her mother that she wants the racket, but her mother tells her that they just don't have enough money now to buy it. But our player refuses to give up on her dream. She trusts that she will get that racket, whether it is by working, or asking her grandparents for money or begging her mom. Do you know what happens if this continues?

You are right. The kid will get that racket.

This can happen with a racket, a tennis scholarship like I explained already, even making it to the top of the International Tennis Federation, the Women's Tennis Association, or Association of Tennis Professionals rankings.

But the space for doubt is unacceptable.

Your idea or goal must be extremely clear. You don't have to worry much about how you achieve it, because the Universe, energy, or if you are a believer, God will do things for you if you truly believe you can do it.

> "When you want something, all he universe conspires in helping you to achieve it." – **Paulo Coelho**

What did Jesus say about faith?

> "THEN THE DISCIPLES CAME TO JESUS IN PRIVATE AND ASKED, "WHY COULDN'T WE DRIVE IT OUT?" HE REPLIED, "BECAUSE YOU HAVE SO LITTLE FAITH. TRULY I TELL YOU, IF YOU HAVE FAITH AS SMALL AS A MUSTARD SEED, YOU CAN SAY TO THIS MOUNTAIN, 'MOVE FROM HERE TO THERE,' AND IT WILL MOVE. NOTHING WILL BE IMPOSSIBLE FOR YOU." – *Matthew 17:20 NIV*

Napoleon Hill says the following about faith: "Faith is the head chemist of the mind. When faith is blended with the vibration of thought, the subconscious mind instantly picks up the vibration, translates it into spiritual equivalent, and transmits it to the infinite Intelligence, as in the case of prayer."

Now, based on research and our limited knowledge about how this Universe works, maybe this can prove why some people get cured from serious diseases after continued prayer and unwavering faith. Otherwise, how can you explain miracles?

> "Imagination and faith are the secrets of creation."
> - **Neville Goddard**

I cannot say I am right, but my assumption is that since Jesus was the Son of God, the Creator of the Universe, then Jesus could manipulate the physical laws and perform thousands of miracles. He knew about energy and how we all are connected. He knew exactly what to do to accomplish the unimaginable in fractions of a second.

I think most people use these concepts to achieve worldly goals. However, we should be aware of the ultimate goal and purpose, which is going back to our main source, God.

If God is our final purpose, then I believe also we should keep Him in our minds at all times in the same way we keep in our mind material purposes such as winning and achieving goals, buying a house, reaching sales quotas, increasing the number of customers, reaching Grand Slam finals, etc.

> *"Whatever we plant in our subconscious mind and nourish with repetition and emotion will one day become reality." - **Earl Nightingale***

You can also see how this law works technically. When you tell a player a compliment about something he just did, you create in him or her a positive emotion and thought and this creates a new reality in him. Awesome forehand Mike! Your forehand reminds me of Del Potro's forehand!! Keep it up. Then you show him a video of Delpo hitting some forehands and the kid will start thinking with images how he looks. You can also make a video of himself and compare it with Delpo's so he can see the little differences. The student will start focusing and thinking about his forehand looking like Delpo's every time he hits. He will start being conscious about it and proud of it. IF this continues and you continue to promote and motivate that specific forehand, the player will end up hitting and striking the ball with a lot of similarities to Delpo.

The player's thoughts, FEELINGS and actions will create something new. Those three things create our live and personalities. The way we think, the way we feel and the way we act. Therefore, if you want to change your life, game, results, then you need to generate new ideas, thoughts that will create new activities and finally these will generate new and more positive feelings and emotions. Emotions are the result of memories, actions, or thoughts. Emotions and feelings are a good thermometer that tells you how are you doing in life and in tennis. I will repeat again. Emotions and Feelings are KEY for you to move into higher levels of tennis or life but they are connected with your thoughts and actions.

Think about that for a while...

It's not about Force. It's about Feeling.
This is a part of the book that may be even more important than most chapters because feelings are way stronger than thoughts. When you see someone you haven't seen in years and you give them a hug, you can cry without even thinking anything. It's a natural reaction that we have been blessed to have. Feelings and Emotions are powerful.

Before you continue reading this chapter, I recommend watching the movie "The Legend of Bagger Vance" and listen very carefully to the part where Will Smith talks to Junuh about his grip and shots. If you cannot watch it now, then pay much attention to the following Quote from the movie.

"Look with soft eyes. See the place where the tides and the seasons, the turning of the Earth all come together, where everything that is becomes one. You got to seek that place with your soul Junuh. Seek it with your hands, don't think about it, feel it" – **The Legend of Bagger Vance**

I really like this concept and I teach it to my students. When it comes to tennis, it's probably hard to remember for most people because the sport is very technically and physically demanding, but nothing should be executed based on force.

This concept applies for every technical, physical or even mental changes in tennis and you can apply the concept outside the sport also.

If you don't agree, I challenge you to force a technical change to your professional, junior or even recreational player and see what happens. Force your kids to study harder or force them not to go out to party and see the results. Force is never the best way of doing things.

For example, when you have a kid that has learn to serve with a grip other than continental grip, generally speaking, they hold the new grip very tight because they don't want to make a mistake. When they are executing the serve, the hand changes position to the old grip, even though they are holding it very tight.

Most coaches, when they want to teach a new grip, show the kid the different lines on the grip, the knuckles, and where are they supposed to be located. For that reason, the players keep watching their hand and grip before or after every serve to see if they are holding it right.

I have learned after years of coaching and observing that the best way to help a player change a grip is by first asking them NOT to see the grip at all. Then by asking them to feel where the right grip should be located and moving the hand slowly until they find the right spot. Once they have found it by THEMSELVES they need to start hitting shots, but with the condition of holding the racket as lightly as possible. I tell them they should hold it like if they have a bird in their hands. If you squeeze too tight, the bird will get killed, but if you keep it too lose, the bird will fly away. When they start trying to follow these directions, it is imperative to take time to stop and check if the player's hand, arm or body are tight. If they are, give them direction again so they can relax, and you will see how quickly they can change.

Another example is when you ask a player to change their preparation or follow through or stance. Generally speaking, you will need to show them in a video what they are doing "wrong" in order for them to try the new motion. However, if the process stops there and you just repeat the new motion, the change will probably come but it will take a long time.

However, if you ask the player to FEEL where the racket is in a specific moment of the stroke and ask them to stop and check, they will realize their feeling has to improve. When they start feeling where the racket is located, or the shoulder or feet or anything, they will recognize the needed change and things will improve very fast.

Make an experiment with your child not even on the tennis court but at home. Let's say they are arguing or fighting with their sibling. You can choose to punish them and give them a speech about not being physical with each other and so on. Or you can sit them close to you, give them a hug and tell them to relax and to treat their sibling with respect and love.

Once they are calm, give them a kiss and tell them you trust they will do better next time. Trust me, with time you will see which one is more effective. **It is NEVER about force, it's ALWAYS about feeling**.

Also you know that relationships or friendships do not work when you force things. Try to meet a girl and force her to give you her number and see if she agrees. Try to force someone to love you and probably over time you will push them away from you. On the contrary, if you understand and feel your partner's emotions, they will get closer to you, the connection and magnetism will increase, and things will flow better. It's

Not about Force, It's about FEELING.

> *"The less effort, the faster and more powerful you will be."* – **Bruce Lee**

If a kid has been raised in an environment where he was physically abused, saw drugs, violence, and so, the way to that kid is NOT by punishing his mistaken actions. It is by giving him love and understanding repetitively until he believes and FEELS people love him and he can trust them. It's never about force, it's always about feeling.

And when it comes to competing, it is easy to tell your player what to do strategically speaking. But once the match is on, different situations will arise and the strategy you asked for is not applicable many times and the player will have to make decisions and adjust based on experience, instinct or feeling. What feels best usually is the right path to take. I believe good decision making is based on feeling, whether it is to hit a passing shot down the line, cross court, serve and volley or commit to a new career, business project, or employment. When you feel the situation, the right decision will show up. It is important to feel without fear because fear can blind you. Federer, I believe, is almost the perfect example of feeling. From the decisions he makes inside, outside the court, his scheduling, picking his fitness trainer, how he approaches interviews, criticism, etc. He Feels and follows his instinct and inner voice to make decisions about his career. **"It's not about Force, It's about Feeling."**

> *"I was aware of how incredible the match was. Unfortunately there had to be a winner. From my point of view many left feeling sorry for me instead of being happy for Rafa. Which hurts." – **Roger Federer***

Notice all the key words Roger uses on the quote. Aware, point of view, feeling, happy, hurts. In this quote, he gives us a great lesson for life, not just for tennis. This is what a big part of this book is all about. Being aware, feelings, points of views, emotions.

The closer you are to your emotions and the more aware you are of them, the more positive emotions you can create. If this happens, you can mix your positive emotions with your positive thoughts and goals. Then you can start materializing your dreams because you will be more connected to this gigantic energy field that transforms things.

Very successful people understand these rules and know that our emotions and thoughts can create, and that we all are connected and aligned with pure energy, which some call God, or the Universe, a Force, a Source, etc.

I truly think that when you do not force things, you become a force. The only force we should use is our inner force. That force that classic or ancient martial artist used to talk about. The famous Qi, life's force or the intangible but powerful energy flow.

9

CHAPTER

Your Internal Power (IP)

1) Inner Talk & Inner Motivation
2) Quantum Frame Work (Tennis & Life)
3) We think with Images
4) Train your Subconscious Mind
5) Conclusion

Inner Talk

We already talked about the power of focusing on something so much that if you do, then the chances of getting them are pretty high.

How many times have you been aware of your inner talk inside or outside the court?

I have played tennis and competed and sometimes I can assure you my inner talk has been pretty bad. I have criticized myself and even insulted myself. Doing that, does no good to us and we all can agree with that.

Most people use their inner talk negatively not only on the court but outside of it and during all their daily activities such as work, family time, during school and so on.

- I double faulted. That's awful.
- My fitness stinks and I'm getting tired.

- My forehand is so bad!
- I'm so dumb! My boss will not like my proposal
- I just messed up that easy overhead and I looked stupid!
- No one likes me and they don't understand me.
- I'm not good enough!

I can give several examples but you get my point.

Have you ever wonder what would happened if the negative inner talk stops and we start focusing ONLY on motivating ourselves, talking nice to ourselves, giving love to ourselves?

That's what I call:

Inner Motivation

The majority of human beings never get to a point where they know consciously what their inner talk is. They go through life like lost sheep.

Start by writing the good things you want to say about yourself. Make a list, then choose a specific time of the day when you will repeat and concentrate on the list. It can be right after you wake up, before lunch and before you go to sleep. It's almost like praying.

- I'm doing so well! This list will take me to higher levels.
- I'm starting to execute my strokes better!
- My serve looks way better than 2 months ago. I've improved a lot!
- I'm so blessed to be training and competing! Life is amazing..!
- My boss will give me great feedback!
- God will always provide to my family with what we need.
- If I'm positive, I will attract only positive people to my life.
- I'm doing my best every day and I will be rewarded sooner than later.

I think it is easy to see and be honest to ourselves and accept that we do not motive ourselves very often or probably never. We always need someone else to do that for us. Coaches, Parents, Managers, Teammates, etc.

But in reality **WE HAVE** the power to make the change and to create a gigantic positive effect on ourselves by *changing our inner talk and converting it to inner motivation.*

I know I have said this already in the book but **it is imperative we learn to think**. And in order to do that, first we have to learn to be aware of what are we thinking.

It would be nice to live completely in the present and not think but we have a brain that works extremely fast and is not that simple to make it go quiet. For that reason I have built this Frame Work that will allow you to transform not only your way of thinking but it can transform your life.

I think I read once that a negative thought in your mind is like a virus in a computer. As soon as you detect it, you have to erase it. If not, the Virus will gain momentum and then it is harder to get rid of it. Therefore, as soon as you detect a negative thought, it is time to use your antivirus, stop it and then delete it completely from the root.

Choose to think something better that will move you to a higher and positive frequency.

I call the graph below QUANTUM THINKING FRAMEWORK. It will help if you use it. Make sure you make a copy and you have it close to you at all times until you build the good habit of thinking correctly. I will share initially just the concept graph and then a more practical example graph.

QUANTUM THINKING FRAMEWORK. (Starts with a negative thought) Low Frequency

High Frequency Vibrations

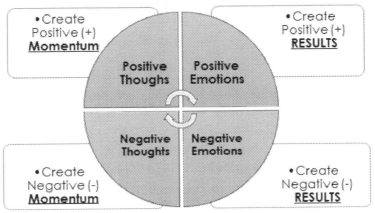

Tennis Thinking Quantum Framework:

High Frequency Vibrations

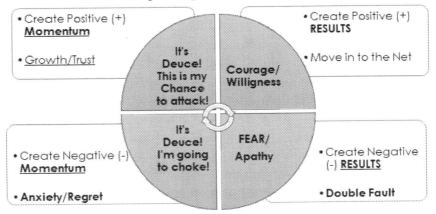

Low Frequency Vibrations

Life Practical Quantum Framework

High Frequency Vibrations

High Frequency Vibrations

- Create Positive (+) **Momentum**
- Growth/Confidence

Here is my chance to start fresh!

COURAGE/ Willigness

- Create Positive (+) **RESULTS**
- Find a new Job, Eat Healthy, Stop Smoking

- Create Negative (-) **Momentum**
- Anxiety/Regret

I will fail again. People dont trust me

FEAR/ Apathy

- Create Negative (-) **RESULTS**
- Keep the same job, Eat junk food or Smoke ciggars

Low Frequency Vibrations

We Think in Images.

If you drive a car to work every morning, I can assure you that sometimes you arrived to your office and you don't even remember how you did it. You don't remember the stop signs or turns and so on because you were thinking about a presentation you will deliver to your employees or you were thinking about home issues or you were remembering what a great movie night you had with your kids and so on.

We are so focused in those memories or in the future, that we actually see our thoughts become reality. We SEE the images of our thoughts remembering or assuming what will happen during other activities.

The same thing happen when we are exercising or when we are watching TV commercials or even when we are talking to someone that is boring and our mind goes somewhere else.

The challenge here is that the majority of people go throughout the day having these images in the mind but most of them are not conscious about them and they allow the brain to control them completely. They do not know how to direct the focus to specific images they want to see proactively.

Most people are in autopilot and it's important to train yourself so most of the time you are seeing the images you want and not the images that just appeared from nowhere.

It's easy to see that we think in images, right? So if this is accurate, then visualizing like some Olympians do, makes more sense immediately. Re-enacting over and over again in our Minds the same new stroke, new motion, new goal, new accomplishment is a MUST and we MUST do it with images.

For that reason, I recommend having a scheduled routine like I mentioned already at least 3 times a day when you see yourself accomplishing what you want in detail over and over again. Whether it's a nice loading position on your serve, a small forehand preparation, a consistent toss in the serve, feeling confident during match points, moving to the net with calm and good timing, winning a tournament, reaching the top 100 or top 10 in the world, getting a new job, building a new house, the IMAGES have to be in your MIND constantly and you have to train yourself to see those images all the time.

The more you see them, the more attainable they will become. You need outstanding discipline to do this and that discipline is the difference between successful people and the rest of the population.

We train our strokes every day and we need to train our Minds, every day also.

Train your Subconscious Mind

The topic about training the subconscious mind is not new at all. A lot of people have had access to this information since the 1800's or way before.

For example, famous and classic actress, Angela Lansbury was interviewed by Claude M. Bristol because he was writing his book "The Magic of Believing" which I recommend reading and this is what

Angela said after he asked her about how she goes about tapping her subconscious mind.

"Heavens! I don't want to sound stuffy and high-brow, but it's really simple. If you tell yourself over and over again that there's no limit to the creative power within you, that's about all there is to it."

Then when she was asked about the suggestibility of the subconscious she said:

"Oh that! Well, when you're about to drop off to sleep, just tell yourself that tomorrow's the day you've got to surpass anything you did today. Bearing in mind and actual mental picture of the situation is even better. If you're scheduled to do a screen test, for example, you *see* yourself acting-out that test better than anyone's ever done it before. Act it like mad in your mind! Be Duse; be Bernhardt! In your mental picture, be the best there is! And when the actual test comes off you find, often to your surprise, that you're acting better than you know how."

Source: "Magic Of Believing" – Claude M. Bristol

I believe all this is true not just because I've studied this topic for the last 14-16 years but also I'm a man of Faith and that's exactly the meaning of Faith. To believe in something without actually having it infront of you. Believing with no actual physical facts or proof.

If you belive in God and have read the new testament, then probably you know what happened when Jesus resurected. Some apostles saw him and Thomas didn't. Thomas told the witnesses that in order to believe them, first he would need to put his hands in Jesus wounds. When Jesus appeared, Thomas said to him, "My Lord and my God!"

Source: New Testament – John 20:28 (New International Version)

Then Jesus told him, "Because you have seen me, you have believed; blessed are those who have not seen and yet have believed"

Source: Source: New Testament – John 20:28 (New International Version)

If you understand this topic, then you will believe and understand my entire book. You will see how not only a tennis stroke, strategy or results can change but also how your life will change.

FAITH is Key in order to comprehend my book and to change your game, your coaching, your parenting, your life.

CONCLUSION

> *"It's very important how you think. Actually, you can destroy yourself or you can create yourself by the manner and quality of your thoughts." – **Norman Dr. Vincent Peale***

I heard on a video once from Dr. Norman Vincent Peale that "Positive thinkers are not afraid of problems" He explains in different ways why but to keep it simple, he says Positive thinkers are not afraid because they KNOW there is always a solution to a problem and also because they know they will end up stronger after overcoming and dealing with the problems. Later on Dr. Peale says the following:

"The individual that thinks negatively does a very dangerous thing because he constantly sends out from his mind, negative animations that activate the World around him negatively."

Source: **https://www.youtube.com/watch?v=EQHI9CV-EdU**

The words Dr. Peale shared in the paragraph above cover most of the topics I've developed in this book.

It is my goal to bring awareness not only to the sport of tennis but all sports and life in general. I'm confident that if you read this book with a positive and opened mind, your life can change and you can impact positively the life of others.

I'm hopeful now you can start focusing on all the good things you have as a player and person and not on what you lack. Focus now on what you can create and what you can improve instead of your mistakes and limitations.

Join me in this purpose, practice on a daily basis your faith, what you believe about yourself and others. Practice every day to improve your thoughts and slowly but surely become an expert on the way you think. It will not only improve your game or the way you teach or parent but it will improve your life.

You can also practice proactively about what you want to imagine & feel. Everything starts by imagining something. It has been proven already in laboratories that through imagination and feeling people can move AI objects such as a metal Robotic hand.

That's why Einstein said that imagination is more important than knowledge.

He knew your ideas, thoughts that are not tangible, can become tangible. I heard once Neville Goddard said "**Imagine the Feeling of the Wish Fulfilled**". That's the magical trick for everything. If you can imagine internally what you want and you believe blindly, you can achieve it. You will receive it.

I truly believe he is right and saying the truth because if you remember the words from Matthew 7:7 then you know it is not Goddard or me saying this. It is written in the scriptures and it's a **DIVINE LAW**.

Imagine executing these concepts with your students, players, children, parents, friends or coaches consistently. You can create magic every day. We can become alchemist of our own lives and use free will in the best way possible

I'm sure by now, you are starting to see the World a bit different than how you saw it previously before reading this book and that was exactly what I intended.

Let's be thankful for what we have and let's start focusing on helping and serving people with nice words, thoughts and expectations from them.

When our purpose is clear and pure, good things will happen automatically. I know the sport of tennis can benefit from this. Kids, families, coaches and many people not related to tennis can benefit also.

Let's focus on growing personally, lifting other people positively, working as a team and making this magnificent sport even better than what it is now.

It's all about our MUSTARD SEED!
God Bless|

Printed in the United States
By Bookmasters